EXPLORING SPORTS SERIES

SOFTBALL

about the authors

Marian E. Kneer, Professor of Physical Education, University of Illinois, Chicago Circle Campus, received her PhD from the University of Michigan. Dr. Kneer has had a long association with softball as a player in four ASA World Softball Championships, a member of The Joint International Rules Committee on Softball, a writer of numerous softball articles for the former Division of Girls and Women's Sports, and as a consultant for several softball filmstrips. She has had extensive experiences as a high school physical education teacher and as a softball coach. Presently, Dr. Kneer is a physical education curriculum and instruction specialist and is coauthor of the book *Physical Education Instruction Techniques: An Individualized Humanistic Approach*, published by Prentice-Hall.

Charles McCord, having achieved success in teaching, coaching, and competitive sports, again joins force as coauthor with Dr. Kneer in this revision.

After earning his degree from Eastern Illinois University, he both taught and coached for two years at the high school level. For eighteen years he has officiated competitive sports on both the high school and college level. During this time, he has conducted clinics overseas on softball for the men and women of the United States Armed Forces.

Besides his teaching and coaching accomplishments, he managed the nationally famous women's softball team, Lettes, of Caterpillar-Sunnyland and Pekin, Illinois, from 1947-72. During his tenure, the team qualified for the national tournament nineteen times.

Since 1952 he has held the position of State Softball Commissioner for the Illinois Amateur Softball Association and is also the chairperson of the National Hall of Fame Selection Committee. He has held this position since 1958.

Mr. McCord is a member of the Pan-American Committee for Softball and assisted in writing the procedure for selecting the players to represent the United States teams.

EXPLORING SPORTS SERIES

SOFTBALL

Marian E. Kneer
Charles L. McCord

wcb
Wm. C. Brown Publishers
Dubuque, Iowa

Consulting Editor
Physical Education
Aileene Lockhart
Texas Woman's University

Physical Education Activities
Evaluation Materials Editor
Jane A. Mott
Texas Woman's University

Illustrations by E. Jane Beals
Interior photos by Jon Cunningham

Library of Congress Catalog Card Number: 84-73459
ISBN 0-697-00749-9

Printed in the United States of America
10 9 8 7 6 5 4 3 2 1

contents

preface

The trade edition of SOFTBALL includes information relating to technique changes, rule changes, equipment changes and a general up-dating and refinement of the coverage and illustrations. The *Home Savers Softball Team* of Aurora, Illinois, one of the top ASA Fast Pitch teams in the United States served as models for the new photographs.

The purposes of this book are to assist all softball players in acquiring the knowledge and skills necessary for playing fast or slow pitch softball; to provide instructors, coaches and managers with substantive information about softball and suggestions for structuring meaningful and productive learning experiences; and, to aid interested players and fans to learn how to umpire and keep score. Emphasis has been placed on skill analysis, error correction, values of softball and its place in our culture. Individual and group practice suggestions are included to foster improvement in performance.

Self-evaluation questions are distributed throughout the book. They represent typical examples of the kinds of understanding and levels of skill that the reader should be acquiring in progressing toward mastery of softball. The player should not only answer the printed questions but should pose additional ones as a self-check on learning. Since the order in which the content of the book is read is a matter of individual choice, the questions are not positioned according to the presentation of given topics. In some instances the reader may be unable to respond fully and accurately to a question without reading more extensively or gaining more playing experience. From time to time the reader should return to such troublesome questions until sure of the answers or proficient in the skills called for, as the case may be.

what softball is like

1

Instructional Objectives

The learner will be able to—

1. distinguish softball from baseball,
2. differentiate between fast-pitch and slow-pitch softball,
3. understand the general conduct of a softball game,
4. identify the playing areas of an official field,
5. identify equipment necessary for playing softball.

Softball is a variation of baseball that was originated by George Hancock of Chicago, Illinois in 1887 to permit the popular game of baseball to be played indoors. He devised smaller playing dimensions to accommodate the larger and softer ball. The variation became so popular that the indoor game was brought outdoors and became known by a variety of names such as kittenball or mushball. Recreation agencies found the adaptation to be better suited and more appealing to all ages and both sexes than baseball which required a heavier bat, smaller and harder ball, and a larger playing area. Softball, on the other hand, is played on a smaller diamond with a larger ball and a lighter bat. The pitcher pitches underhand instead of overhand. Base runners may not lead off base until the ball leaves the pitchers hand, and a game consists of seven instead of nine innings. These changes provide a sport which is like baseball but can be played in a smaller area by men, women, and children. It has become basically an amateur sport; whereas baseball includes professional as well as amateur play. Softball has become the largest participating sport in the United States.[1]

Softball is a game for everyone. Power is required to hit the ball, yet accuracy in placing the ball so that a fielder cannot reach it can make up for lack of power. The varied playing situations require quick, intelligent decisions. The game calls for individual and team effort. Basic skills are throwing, catching, running, and hitting. The game demands strenuous effort and yet provides suf-

1. *Softball a Game for Everyone,* (Oklahoma City: Amateur Softball Association of America, 1977), p. 2.

ficient rest periods. The equipment is relatively inexpensive, and the rules are easily adapted to various playing situations. Softball is one of the safest sports for participants of any age.

Informal softball is played extensively with rules modified by the participants to suit the situation at picnics, in parks, in backyards, or on the streets. The thrill of catching a ball or striking an object with a bat is sought by many. The game is most often played officially by leagues comprised of several teams. These leagues may be sponsored by schools, playgrounds, recreation departments, churches or industrial organizations. The highly skilled players perform on teams that are usually sponsored by a business or industrial organization. The teams often travel considerable distances to seek comparable competition. The Amateur Softball Association has drawn up rules governing play for teams that wish to affiliate and to compete in metropolitan, state, regional, national, and international competition.

There are several variations of the game: fast-pitch softball, which is considered the standard game; twelve-inch slow-pitch and sixteen-inch slow-pitch softball.

The game of fast-pitch softball requires nine players on a team and ten if a designated hitter is to be used. Each team assigns players to certain defensive positions. These are pitcher, catcher, first baseman, second baseman, third baseman, shortstop, left fielder, center fielder, right fielder. The designated hitter does not play a defensive position but rather is assigned to bat for one of the defensive players who does not then bat. The players are stationed on a playing field that has a clear and unobstructed area within a radius of 225 feet from home plate between the foul lines. The batter stands at home plate and tries to hit a ball that is delivered by the pitcher. If the batter succeeds, he tries to reach first base and eventually advance around the diamond until he returns to home plate. The players in the field try to prevent runners from scoring. Each time a runner crosses home plate, a run is scored. The team with the most runs after seven innings of play is the winner. Pitching dominates fast-pitch softball when it is played by highly skilled players.

The pitcher must deliver the ball underhand. The batter must decide whether he wishes to swing at the pitch. If he does not swing at it, the umpire judges whether the ball was delivered over the plate and between the batter's armpits and the top of his knees when the batter assumes his natural batting stance. This area is called the strike zone. If the pitch is in the strike zone, a strike is called. If it is not, a ball is called. If three strikes are called, the batter is declared out. If four balls are called, the batter is allowed to take first base. The batter attempts to hit the ball so that it will settle on fair ground in the infield or strike fair ground in the outfield. If the batted ball is hit outside of this area it is in foul territory and is called a foul ball. The first two are counted as strikes. When the batter hits the ball into fair territory, he and all other base runners try to reach as many bases as possible.

The defensive team members play positions within the boundary lines of the field and attempt to put batters and base runners out before they are able to complete the circuit of the bases.

Figure 1.1 illustrates the diamond and the defensive areas covered by each player. Outs occur when the batter strikes out, when a fly ball is caught, when

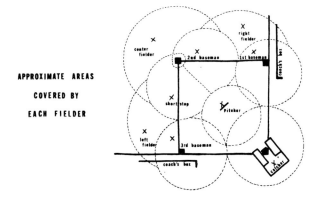

APPROXIMATE AREAS

COVERED BY

EACH FIELDER

Figure 1.1   Diamond and Defensive Stations (Fast Pitch)

the base is touched with the ball before the runner reaches it if he is forced to run because of a succeeding runner, and when a runner is touched with the ball before reaching a base. Three outs retire the batting team. The fielding team is then given a chance to bat and to score runs. When each team has had a turn at bat, an inning has been completed.

Slow-pitch softball has in recent years shown tremendous growth. The major difference from fast-pitch softball is evident in the name itself. The pitcher is restricted to delivering the ball at a moderate speed with a perceptible arc from the time it leaves his hand until it reaches approximately three feet in front of home plate. Base runners may not steal bases, and a team consists of ten players. The extra player is called a short fielder and may play anywhere on the field but usually plays between center field and second base. Designated hitters are not allowed. Bunting is illegal. Another popular variation of the game is the use of a sixteen-inch ball with slow pitch rules.

Slow pitch softball provides more action since a slower pitched ball makes hitting the ball easier. The extra player is necessary to eliminate place-hitting over second base. The unobstructed playing area is extended twenty-five feet for women and fifty feet for men. Batters dominate the game and even former professional baseball players enjoy playing slow pitch softball.

The minimum equipment necessary to play softball officially is a ball and a bat. However, players usually wear gloves or mitts. Catchers must wear masks and women catchers chest protectors. Batting helmets are becoming more frequently used. Shoes which provide traction with metal or rubber spikes attached to the sole and heel of the shoes are considered essential. Uniforms are optional but are often worn by teams in leagues and in highly skilled competition. More information about equipment is provided in Chapter Two.

The game of fast-pitch or slow-pitch softball provides enjoyment and challenge for persons of both sexes, all ages, and varied skill levels. A great deal of force and control is necessary to hit or throw the ball within the limits of the playing space. Players must learn to absorb that force in order to catch or stop the ball. Timing and flow are integral aspects of the game. Timing is needed for executing plays or swinging at the pitched ball. Flow of movement is essential for combining a series of skills for a single execution, such as pitching or executing a double play.

How do slow and fast pitch softball compare in the following: number of players; amount of action in the game; delivery of pitches; base running, and bunting regulations?

REFERENCES

DOBSON, MARGARET, and SISLEY, BECKY. *Softball for Girls.* New York: Ronald Press, 1971. Chapters 1 and 2.
NOREN, ARTHUR T. *Softball with Official Rules.* 3rd ed. New York: Ronald Press, 1966.
SCHUNK, CAROL. "Tenth Man Theme." *1972-74 Softball Guide.* Washington, D.C.: Division of Girls and Women's Sports, American Association for Health, Physical Education and Recreation.
SEIDEL, BEVERLY; BILES, FAY; FIGBY, GWEN; and NEUMANN, BONNIE. *Sport Skills: A Conceptual Approach to Meaningful Movement.* Dubuque, Ia.: Wm. C. Brown Co. Publishers, 1975.
Softball, A Game for Everyone, Oklahoma City, Oklahoma: Amateur Softball Association, 1977.
SMITH, C. J. "Try a Little Slow Pitch." *1972-74 Softball Guide.* Washington, D.C.: Division of Girls and Women's Sports, American Association for Health, Physical Education and Recreation.

facts for enthusiasts

2

Enthusiasts need to know the kind of equipment to purchase and how to care for it. In addition, information about the possibilities of participation in tournaments will enhance a player's appreciation of the game.

Instructional Objectives

The learner will be able to —

1. select and care for equipment,
2. appreciate the wide acceptance of softball.

SELECTION AND CARE OF EQUIPMENT

The minimum equipment necessary to play softball officially is a ball and a bat. Bases may be makeshift, and official dimensions modified.

Bats

The rules permit a variety of materials to be used in manufacturing official bats: wood, wood laminated, plastic, bamboo, and metal. In addition, there are several unofficial plastic bats that are hollow, lightweight and do not present a hazard to students or to gym floors. A wide selection of bats with differing size grips and barrels should be available. The bat is made of one piece of hardwood of formed from woods bonded together with plastic, bamboo, or metal. The surface must be smooth and free of burrs, rivets, or other hazards. It is not more than 34 inches long or more than 2⅛ inches in diameter at its largest part and has a safety grip of cork, tape, or composition material.

Choose a bat that feels balanced and seems to be the proper weight for you to swing with power and whip. A heavy, tapered bat is often used by power hitters. The "bottleneck" bat is used for sharp hits out of the infield or for bunting. Bats made from ash woods tend to be lighter than hickory bats. At the end of the season, or periodically during a season if the bat is used often, treat the bat with boiled linseed oil and store in a dry room at an even temperature. Moisture will cause the bat to splinter. The aluminum bat has gained in popularity and is becoming the kind most often used by players.

Balls

The ball must be 12⅜ inches in circumference and six ounces in weight. The core of the ball is composed of kapok or a mixture of cork and rubber. This core is dipped in rubber cement and covered with horsehide or synthetic material.

Softballs are closely controlled by the rules as to weight, diameter, contents, cover, and stitching. Be certain when buying softballs that they are marked "Official Softball." The brand name of the balls you purchase depends upon personal choice. Most players like to play with a ball that "feels" light; however, these balls often are not durable.

Fleece balls and plastic balls are recommended for primary-age children, but in junior high school, regular fast-pitch softballs should be used. If the ball seems too hard, a rubber-covered, soft softball may be more desirable. Teams should use regulation softballs. Tests are made each year by the Amateur Softball Association Equipment Standards Committee to determine conformity to the rules.

Gloves and Mitts

There are many styles of gloves and mitts. Mitts do not have fingers. Individual differences in hand size and comfort of the glove will determine the style you purchase. Only the catcher and the first baseman may wear mitts, and the rules spell out the specific regulations concerning their pattern. Most players prefer a baseball glove with a large pocket to gloves specially constructed for softball use. Baseball mitts do not work well for catcher's mitts. Usually, first basemen's mitts are used by catchers. Padding is not too important in softball gloves or mitts, but the softness of the leather is important. Horse-, cow-, or elkhide are excellent leather coverings. The palms should be oiled or greased. At the end of the season, mitts and gloves should be oiled and stored with a ball or a wad of paper wrapped in the pocket.

Why do you suppose aluminum bats are often preferred over wood bats?

Masks and Protectors

Masks must be worn by catchers; body protectors also must be worn by women catchers. Softball masks are made much lighter than baseball masks. They can be purchased with sponge rubber padding or with hair padding covered with leather. Both are excellent, and the selection is a matter of individual preference. Body protectors should be made especially for softball and be only waist long. Light-colored duck filled with kapok is the material commonly used for protec-

Figure 2.1   Softball Equipment

tors. Some catchers prefer to wear shin guards and throat protector flaps on their masks.

Shoes

Most players prefer to wear spiked shoes for better traction on the playing ground. Shoes should conform to official rules as to construction. Soft leather is desirable for greater comfort. Shoes of canvas or leather, with rubber or metal spikes not more than three-quarters inch in length and attached to the sole and heel of the shoe, are worn to provide good traction.

Bases, Home Plate, Pitcher's Plate

The regulation home plate is five-sided and made of rubber. The pitcher's plate is constructed of wood or rubber, twenty-four inches long and six inches wide. For women, the pitcher's plate is placed forty feet from home plate; for men and women playing slow pitch the distance is forty-six feet. Bases covered with canvas or other suitable material are fifteen inches square. They are placed sixty feet apart and are fastened in place.

In official games, home and pitcher's plates are rubber, and the bases are made with a canvas cover. Official play requires that all bases and plates be secured to the ground.

THE GAME TODAY

For many years softball was a recreational sport in the United States. Today it has a home in almost every country in the world. Over eighteen million adults and youngsters in the United States and over five million in other parts of the world play softball. In 1965 the first world championships were played in Australia. Since that time, championships have been held in Asia, the South Pacific, the Caribbean, Europe, Japan, and the United States. Women have shown outstanding interest and have given leadership in promoting softball. Don Porter, executive director of the Amateur Softball Association, states: "There is hardly a man or woman in the United States who didn't at one time play softball."[1] Playing field facilities are insufficient to fill the demand for playing softball, especially slow-pitch softball. Rules are printed in fifteen different languages.

The Amateur Softball Association (ASA) is organized to promote softball and to provide clinics and information designed to improve play as well as to organize tournaments on a local, district, state, regional, national, and world basis. More than 100,000 teams are involved in ASA adult programs for both fast-pitch and slow-pitch softball. Each year more than a thousand invitational and championship tournaments are conducted at all levels of skill and for both sexes. The ASA Youth Program involves over five hundred thousand children.

In 1957 the Amateur Softball Association developed a Softball Hall of Fame. Selections are made on the basis of documented evidence of outstanding performance and contributions to the game on a national level. The headquarters for the Amateur Softball Association and the Softball Hall of Fame are located in Oklahoma City, Oklahoma. In addition to the above services the ASA provides the following:

> Aids and clinics for umpires, coaches, and players
> Assistance in local league organization and play
> Publications (rules, guides, monthly newspaper, and national magazine)
> Free literature and instructional films

The National Association for Girls and Women's Sports (NAGWS) and the National Association for Sport and Physical Education of the American Alliance for Health, Physical Education and Recreation promote softball in educational institutions. The NAGWS sponsors a Softball Committee that biannually publishes a Softball Guide with instructional articles, officiating information, rules, and media resources. Softball is usually included in the physical education curriculum from elementary school through college.

1. Don E. Porter, "Softball—Past, Present and Future," *Journal of Health, Physical Education Recreation* 42 (May 1971):36-37.

Figure 2.2   Softball Hall of Fame

Several attempts have been made to professionalize the game. An attempt was made for women in the late forties and fifties and again for both men and women in the late seventies.

REFERENCES

ASA Softball. Oklahoma City, Okla.: Amateur Softball Association (nationally circulated magazine).
Balls and Strikes. Oklahoma City, Okla.: Amateur Softball Association (monthly newspaper).
National Association for Girls and Women's Sports. Softball Guide. Washington, D.C.: American Alliance for Health, Physical and Recreation (published bianually).
Softball Rules Guide. Oklahoma City, Okla.: Amateur Softball Association (published yearly).

language and lore of the game

3

Instructional Objectives

The learner will be able to—

1. appreciate and understand the history of softball,
2. understand and apply common softball terms.

The concept of striking an object and reaching a destination before being "put out" can be traced to England. Early games based on this concept were called "Rounders" or "Town Ball." The early colonists adapted "Rounders" into a game called "Old One Cat." Folklore credits Abner Doubleday in 1839 as having scratched the first baseball diamond in the dust at Cooperstown, New York, and outlined general playing rules. It was then that baseball and its many variations started to grow.

Softball is the most famous offspring of baseball, our national pastime. On a Thanksgiving afternoon in 1887 the Chicago Farragut Boat Club devised and played an indoor game similar to baseball. A boxing glove and broom were used as a ball and bat. The afternoon's fun offered promise, a promise fulfilled by George W. Hancock, a member of the club, who developed rules and equipment. He produced a larger, softer ball and a bat with a smaller batting surface.

Early organization of game play began in Minneapolis, Minnesota. Lewis Rober, a member of the municipal fire department, made the first "kittenball," or softball, by hand. The firemen amused themselves by playing with it in their free time. The first softball league was organized in Minneapolis in 1900, and the first published rules covering the sport appeared in Minneapolis in 1906. During the next twenty years the game was played both indoors and outdoors. It was called mushball, kittenball, and pumpkinball. Because the game was less dangerous than baseball, women readily took to it. They started to play the game at almost the same time as men and found that, unlike baseball, they could play it well. The game was called "softball" by Walter A. Hakanson, a YMCA Director from Denver, Colorado, in 1926. That name was officially adopted in 1933.

Since indoor space was not always available, the game began to be played outdoors more and more. Around 1930 Leo H. Fischer and M. J. Pauley of Chicago adapted the game so that it could be played outdoors. They conducted tournaments which were so successful that they were able to convince the 1933 Chicago World's Fair to sponsor a national tournament for men and for women.

Thousands of unemployed adults of the 1932-33 depression years found the game a satisfying way to use excess leisure time. When they finally found employment, they took the game with them and encouraged their employers to sponsor industrial leagues and teams of highly skilled players. The first national tournament pointed up a need for greater organization. In 1934 all organizations sponsoring tournaments met and formed the Amateur Softball Association. At the same time a Joint Rules Committee was formed to standardize rules. Previous to the formation of this committee, the National Recreation Association and the American Physical Education Association published their own set of rules.

The Amateur Softball Association organized softball into city, state, and regional associations as well as industrial, city, and church leagues. Regional champions compete in a national tournament. Early championship teams came from the Midwest. Since that time champions have come from all different parts of the United States. The national fast-pitch men's and women's championship teams compete in a World Championship tournament. Many teams were and still are sponsored by business and industrial concerns. Some of the sponsors of national championship teams are Aetna Insurance Company, AMF, Avco-Lycoming, Briggs Company, IBM, Jax Brewery, Kodak, Raybesto-Manhattan, Sealmaster Company, Sears, Westinghouse, Wilson, Home Savings, Xerox, Zollner Piston Company, and Dow Chemical Company.

During World War II, softball experienced a brief departure from amateur to professional play for some girls and women. It was born out of concern for the restricted baseball activity because of the war. In Chicago a Women's Professional League was formed, and shortly afterward, P. K. Wrigley gave support to a Midwest version of women's professional play in a game that was essentially a blend of softball and baseball. Both of these attempts died shortly after the end of the war.

Fast-pitch softball dominated the game from 1940 to 1960. The tendency for excellent pitching to result in low-scoring games gave rise to increasing interest in two variations of the game: slow-pitch softball with a regular-size ball and slow-pitch softball with a larger-size ball. These variations prohibited base stealing, required the ball to be pitched slowly, and permitted a tenth fielder. Slow-pitch softball attracts about 70 percent of softball participants.

Competition today includes tournaments sponsored by the Amateur Softball Association for non-school participants, by the National High School Athletic Association for high school girls and by the Association for Intercollegiate Athletics for Women for college women. The ASA sponsors national championships for boys and girls and men and women for both fast pitch and slow pitch softball. Softball is played in fifty countries; the world championships involve over twenty countries. The game is included in the Pan-American games and is expected to be accepted as an Olympic game.

As both baseball and softball were played experts developed the game by devising certain playing techniques, and some of their inventions resulted in the formation of new rules. Bill Cummings of Massachusetts developed spins on pitches by the skips and turns he observed when flinging clam shells into the ocean. Paul "Windmill" Watson of Arizona developed the circular windup and the fast pitch. John "Cannonball" Baker of Wisconsin invented the figure eight windup. These developments resulted in increasing the pitching distances and prohibiting some of the windups.

The National Softball Hall of Fame was established by the ASA in 1957 and is located in Oklahoma City, Oklahoma. Both men and women players are eligible to be selected. Over sixty members have been inducted which also includes founders, executives and umpires. Visitors may view the historical development of the game, see the pictures of great players, and obtain information about their achievements. Some of the famous men in the Softball Hall of Fame are Harold Gears, Sam Elliott, Al Linde, Bernie Kampschmidt, Dizzy Kirkendall, Jim Ramage, Clarence Miller, John Baker, Warren Gerber, Hugh Johnson, Bill West, John Hunter, Tom Castle, Ben Crane, Ray Stephenson, Don Ropp, Jim Chambers, John Spring, Jerry Curtis, and Charles Justice. Women members of the Hall of Fame include Amy Peralta, Marie Wadlow, Betty Grayson, Ruth Sears, Nina Korgan, Marjorie Law, Kay Rich, Margaret Dobson, Bertha Tickey, and Gloria May. Slow-pitch "greats" are Myron Reinhardt, Frank DeLuca, and Don Rardin.

COMMON SOFTBALL TERMS

Most of the terms used in softball are taken from baseball. In most cases these terms simply explain the situation or name the person or item. Some of the terms seem to have little relationship to the situation defined, but there is usually some interesting lore about them.

Appeal Play. A violation of the rules that must be called to the umpire's attention for a ruling. Appeal situations result from leaving a base before a fly ball is caught, not touching a base, or batting out of order.

Assist. A fielding credit to a player who helps a teammate make a putout.

Away. The number of outs. "Two away" means the same as "two outs."

Backstop. Another name for the catcher and also the term given to a fence behind home plate.

Back-up. A position taken by a fielder behind the player attempting to field the ball to possibly play the ball if it gets past the first fielder.

Bag. The base.

Balk. A term applied to making a motion to pitch without immediately delivering the ball to the batter. If a balk is committed, a ball is called on the batter, and the base runners are given one additional base.

Base on Balls. When four balls are called on the batter.

Bases Loaded, or *Bases Full.* Base runners on every base.

Batter's Box. An area on each side of home plate that is seven feet long and three feet wide. The batter must stand within that area when batting.

Battery. The pitcher and the catcher. They are given that name because they really are the "power source" for action.

Bean Ball. A ball pitched too close to the batter's head.

Beat Out. To reach a base on a slowly hit ball or a bunt.

Blocked Ball. A batted or thrown ball that is interfered with by someone not officially in the game.

Blooper. A batted ball that arches over the heads of the infielders and drops just in front of the outfielders.

Bobble. Juggling the ball while attempting to catch it.

Box. The batter's area, the catcher's area, and the coaches' area. All are officially measured and described in the rules.

Box Score. The description of the game that is condensed by the use of symbols. This name was given because the scorekeepers are assigned to an area referred to as a box.

Bunt. A weakly tapped ball that is directed toward the foul lines between home plate and first base and home plate and third base.

Change of Pace. The varying of the speed of a pitched ball.

Chopper. A batted ball that bounces high.

Chucker. The pitcher.

Circuit Clout. A home run. The batter "clouts" the ball so far that he can circle all the bases.

Clean the Bases. To hit a home run with base runners on.

Cleanup. The fourth hitter in the batting order. This name is given because he is the best hitter and most able to bring runners home.

Complementary Runner. A temporary substitute runner who is permitted by consent of the opposition. The original runner may return to the game.

Count. The number of called balls and strikes.

Crowd the Plate. Standing close to the plate.

Cut. To swing at the ball.

Cutoff. To intercept a throw for the purpose of throwing out a runner.

Diamond. The area formed by the four bases.

Double Play. Two outs resulting from one batted ball.

Down. Denotes the number of outs—similar to "away."

Earned Run. A run that was scored through offensive play rather than an error.

Error. A defensive misplay.

Extra-base Hit. A batted ball on which the batter reaches more than one base other than on an error.

Fair Ball. Any legally batted ball that is touched or which stops in fair territory between home and first and home and third base, or which lands in fair territory and does not cross the foul line until after it passes first or third base.

Fan. To strike out.

Fielder's Choice. A play in which the fielder elects to put out a base runner rather than the batter.

Fly Ball. A batted ball hit into the air.

Foot in Bucket. The batter steps away from the plate with his forward foot.

Force Out. An out occurring when the defensive player in possession of the ball merely touches the base before the runner, who must move to that base because of the batter's becoming a base runner, reaches it.

Foul Ball. A ball hit outside of fair territory.

Foul Tip. A batted ball that goes directly to the catcher and is caught. A strike is called.

Full Count. Three balls and two strikes.

Fungo. A ball hit by tossing the ball from the hand and then hitting it. Fungo hitting is used to provide fielding practice.

Grand Slam. Home run with the bases loaded. Taken from the bridge term meaning the best you can get.

Groove. The middle of the strike zone.

Grounder. A batted ball that hits the ground as soon as it leaves the bat.

Hit. To take a turn batting or to hit the ball so as to enable the batter to reach first base safely other than on an error or a base on balls.

Hit Away. Batter swinging for a hit rather than a bunt.

Hit Batsman. A batter hit by a pitched ball.

Hit the Dirt. To slide or to pull away from a bean ball.

Hole. Area not covered by a defensive player. Holes result from shifts in positions.

Infield. Fair territory bounded by and including the base paths.

Innings. A division of the game whereby each team has a turn at batting.

Keystone Sack. Second base.

Lay One Down. To bunt.

Line Drive. A batted ball that travels in a straight line.

Mask. Device worn by the catcher and umpires to protect their faces against foul balls or the bat.

Out. The retirement of a batter or base runner during play.

Outfield. The fair territory beyond the infield.

Outside Pitch. Pitched ball that misses the strike zone on the side away from the batter. It is an inside pitch if it misses on the side near the batter.

Overrun. To run beyond the base.

Overthrow. To throw above the baseman or fielder's head.

Pass. A walk.

Passed Ball. A legally pitched ball that the catcher fails to hold.

Pickoff. To trap a runner off base.

Pinch Hitter. A substitute hitter. So named because often he is put in when a team is losing or in a "pinch."

Pinch Runner. A substitute who is put in a game to replace a slow or injured runner on base. The replaced runner is then out of the game.

Pitchout. A pitch purposely thrown wide of the plate so that the batter cannot hit it.

Pop-up. A short, high fly in or near the infield.

Pull Hitter. A hitter who tends to hit the ball too soon and then sharply follows through.

Putout. When a batter or base runner flies or is thrown out.

RBI. Runs batted in.

Relay Man. A player who catches a ball from another fielder for possible additional play or redirection.

Sacrifice. Advancing a runner by forcing play only on the batter.

Scratch Hit. A weak hit.

Shoestring Catch. A low diving catch by an outfielder. This term is used because the fielder literally catches the ball off his shoestrings.

Southpaw. Left-handed pitcher or batter. Most ball fields are laid out with pitcher facing west; thus his left hand would face south.

Squeeze. Advancing a runner from third by bunting.

Steal. To advance to another base after the ball leaves the pitcher's hand and before he is in position to pitch again.

Straight Away. Normal defensive and hitting pattern.

Stuff. Quality and quantity of the types of pitches used by the pitcher.

Texas Leaguer. Weak fly that lands safely.

Tag. To touch a base with the ball in hand before a runner arrives or to touch the runner with ball in hand.

Tally. To score a run.

Triple Play. Three outs resulting from one batted ball.

Walk. Occurs when four balls are called on the batter. He is then entitled to go to first base.

Wild Pitch. An inaccurately delivered pitch that the catcher has little or no chance of stopping.

Wait Out. Strategy by the batter employed to insure hitting only good pitches but especially contrived to obtain a base on balls.

Can you define these softball terms: bobble, blooper, bean ball, stuff, and relay man.

REFERENCES

Amateur Softball Association. *Softball Rules Guide.* Oklahoma City, Okla.

PORTER, DON E. "Softball—The Game Everyone Plays." *Holiday Inn International Magazine* (July-August 1974) :45-46.

offensive skills
4

Softball is a fast-moving game that requires speed in running, agility in fielding, accuracy in hitting and throwing. The degree of mastery in applying these essential fundamentals to specific techniques of batting, fielding, throwing, and baserunning will determine the ultimate enjoyment to be derived from playing the game. Since it takes the ball about one-third to one-half second to reach the batter from the pitcher's hand and about three seconds for a runner to run from one base to another, it is apparent that the defensive team must develop sufficient skill to catch and to throw with speed and precision.

BATTING

Instructional Objectives

The learner will be able to—

1. hit pitched balls into fair territory,
2. bunt pitched balls that will roll slowly in fair territory near the foul line,
3. hit pitched balls into the desired areas,
4. analyze batting errors and apply corrective procedures.

No matter how well you can field, run, or throw, your value to a team will be considerably reduced if you do not have ability in batting. If you can't hit, you can't score, and if you can't score, you can't win. There are many different styles of batting. If one style seems to bring more success than another, adopt that style. The first step is to select a bat which is the proper length, weight, and style for your body-build, strength, and type of swing. Generally, short, small players select lighter and shorter bats, and vice versa for taller and heavier players. The bat should feel balanced in your hands. It should be heavy enough to add force to the swing but light enough to permit wrist wrip action.

There are three types of grips—long, medium, and short or "choke." Regardless of the length of the grip, the bat is held with the hands together and with the fingers and thumbs wrapped around the handle. If you are right-handed, place your right hand above your left hand. The reverse is true for left-handed players. The second joints of the fingers of your top hand should line up somewhere between the second and base joints of the fingers of your lower hand. Grasp th bat firmly but relaxed until you begin the swing.

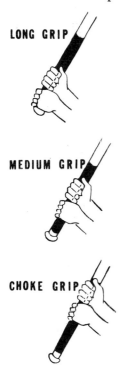

LONG GRIP

Long or power grip. Hands near knob to increase leverage and to add force.

MEDIUM GRIP

Medium or average grip. Lower hand is an inch or two up from the knob to obtain both power and accuracy.

CHOKE GRIP

Choke grip. Lower hand is placed three to four inches from knob to shorten leverage and gain control.

Figure 4.1   Batting Grips

Stance

The distance you should stand from the plate can be measured and adjusted by bending slightly from the waist and placing the top of the bat on the outside corner of the plate while holding the bat with your regular grip. You should feel comfortable and balanced.

1. Stand facing the plate, feet parallel with the ground and shoulder-distance apart.
2. Left shoulder (right-handed batters) and head face the pitcher.
3. Knees should be relaxed and slightly bent.
4. Bat is held off the shoulder.
5. Arms are held away from the body so they are free to move.
6. Forward arm is held fairly level with the ground.
7. Lower back arm a bit to permit better leverage.
8. Eyes on the ball.

Figure 4.2 Batting
Stance

Figure 4.3 Front View
of Stance

Figure 4.4 Side View
of Stance

The Swing

There are many different styles of batting. However, the stride, pivot, and arm action are crucial to successful hitting.

1. Shift weight back as the pitch is released and stride forward about eight to twelve inches with lead foot. The timing of this action depends upon the expected speed of the ball. Keep the rear foot firm. Do not transfer weight forward.
2. Swing bat by rotating shoulders and transfer weight forward as the arms come around.
3. Keep eyes on the ball as you pivot at the hips.
4. Keep hips, shoulders and bat level.
5. Snap wrists just before contact with the ball, roll hands over and follow through.

The swinging action is like a coiling and uncoiling around a central axis, the spine. The swing is a rhythmical progressive movement starting with the pivot of the hips and shoulders, continuing with the arms and wrists. This coiling and uncoiling along with the back arm provides the power while the forward arm gives guidance to the swing. The rear leg supports the initial unleashing of the power and the front leg becomes the support for the transfer of power behind the ball.

Place-hitting   The number or position of base runners as well as the position of the infield often leaves "holes" or openings between the fielders. A clever hit-

Figure 4.5   The Swing

ter knows how to bat into that area. Effective placements of the batted ball can be achieved by adjusting the time that the ball is hit, the position of the feet, and the follow-through of the bat.

If you wish to bat the ball to the left side of the field, try to contact the ball in front of the body in order to shorten the arc of the swing. Your wrists should break sharply, causing a forceful follow-through to "pull" the ball to the side on which you are hitting. To hit the ball to center field, try to contact the ball directly opposite your body and follow through naturally. To hit the ball to right field, try to contact the ball a little past the center of the body; let your follow-through angle the bat to right field. It is also possible to achieve placement of the ball by adjusting your stance, but this method permits the defense to become aware of your intentions and thus take preventive measures. If the pitcher is extremely fast or deceptive, it may not be possible to control the placement of the ball by these measures. In such situations the batter should "go with the pitch." Going with the pitch means that if the ball is outside, it is hit to that side of the field and vice versa. To hit a long fly ball, grip the bat with a

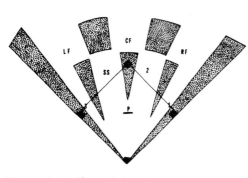

Figure 4.6   Place-Hitting Areas

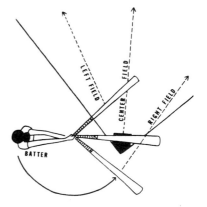

Figure 4.7   Place-Hitting Technique

long grip, swing with full force, and try to follow through slightly upward. To avoid hitting a ground ball, strike only at pitches above the waist.

When the pitcher has a great deal of speed, "choke" your grip on the bat in order to shorten the arc and permit a faster swing. Since this action results in decreased leverage, the power behind the ball will be lessened, but the accuracy of the hit will be increased.

Place-hitting ability is a definite asset to a team. Every good player should develop skill in this advanced technique.

From your observation of softball games, toward which direction do the majority of the hits travel? Do you know why it is preferable to place hit by adjusting your timing rather than your stance?

Hit-and-Run   This technique is used to advance a base runner two or more bases, and at the same time it permits a ground ball, which normally would be fielded, to become a base hit. The hit-and-run play is most often used when there is a runner on first base. As soon as the ball leaves the pitcher's hand the runner on first base runs full speed to the next base. This action forces the second baseman to move to cover second base, thereby opening up a defensive "hole." The batter tries to place the ball into that "hole." Whenever this play is attempted by the offensive team, a gamble is taken that a sharp line drive will not be hit directly to a fielder, which would result in a double or triple play. Hit-and-run skill is difficult to master.

Bunting   Bunting is an essential skill for any fast-pitch softball player. A bunt is a batted ball that is not hit with a full swing. The bat is not swung at the ball but is placed in the way of the ball and allowed to "give" slightly in the hands, thus causing the ball to lose force. This action allows the ball to be placed approximately ten to twenty feet from the plate and as near the base line as possible.

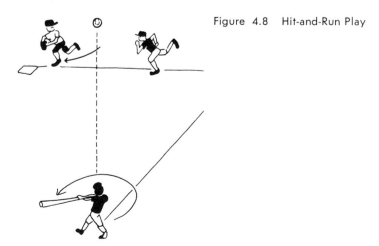

Figure 4.8   Hit-and-Run Play

Figure 4.9 Stance and Sacrifice Bunting

Figure 4.10 Side View of Stance for Sacrifice Bunting

Figure 4.11 Rear View of Stance for Sacrifice Bunting

By taking this grip, what signal have you sent to the defensive team about the distance of your hit?

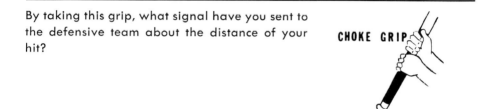

The ball is bunted to advance a baserunner or as an attempt to get a base hit. Bunting to advance a baserunner is called *sacrificing*. The sacrifice bunt draws the first baseman, pitcher and third baseman in toward the plate to field the ball which forces the ball to be thrown to first base thus permitting the baserunner to advance. A variation of the sacrifice bunt is the *squeeze bunt* which is designed to score a baserunner from third base. There are two techniques for bunting for a base hit: *drag bunting* and *push bunting*. Each of these requires surprise, proper placement and a fast sprint to first base to be successful. The drag bunt is placed along the first base line as the batter begins to run to first base. The push bunt is placed between the incoming fielders with enough speed to force the ball by them.

A great deal of the success of the bunt depends on the surprise element; a batter therefore must not assume the bunting position until the ball is about to leave the pitcher's hand. There are three bunting positions for the body.

As the batter strides forward, the body weight should remain over the rear foot. Why is it important to avoid transferring the weight forward with the stride?

Sacrifice bunt.

1. Stand near the front of the batter's box.
2. Move the rear foot in line with the front foot about twelve to eighteen inches apart as the pitcher begins the delivery.
3. Face the pitcher, arms extended forward, bat held at the top of the strike zone, knees and hips slightly bent with weight on both feet.

Drag bunt.

1. Move your feet and arms as they normally move for a full swing.
2. Slide the top hand six to eight inches up the handle just before the ball reaches the plate.
3. Stride toward first base as the ball is contacted.

Push bunt.

1. Move hands and feet as for a drag bunt.
2. Reduce the amount of give and push the ball with enough force between the fielders.

Figure 4.12   The Grip   Figure 4.13   Drag Bunt

Figure 4.14   Push Bunt

Positioning the bat at the top of the strike zone insures hitting the ball downward with the bottom portion of the bat. The batter lowers the level of the bat by bending the knees and hips while keeping the arms extended. The bat should be angled downward to the left, the center, or to the right, depending on where you wish to place the bunt. Low pitches are the easiest to bunt. High, inside pitches are extremely difficult to bunt because the bat must be brought upward, resulting in a tendency to hit up, rather than down on the ball.

Fake Bunting   A fake bunt is often attempted to pull the defense in toward the batter in order to help a base runner steal or to permit the batter to place-hit the ball in the defensive position vacated. Preferably, the ball should be batted just over the first or third baseman's head or into the area vacated by the second baseman or shortstop when he has moved to cover a base. When you are going to bluff a bunt to facilitate a base hit, deliberately move into bunting position but do not hit the ball. On the next pitch momentarily move into bunting position and then bring the bat quickly back for the backswing and swing forcefully forward at the ball. If you are faking a bunt to help a runner steal, simply move into bunting position but do not bunt the ball. This action causes the infield to draw in and forces the shortstop to move to cover second or third, depending on which base is being attempted.

Safety

Batting has two major safety hazards: being hit by the pitched ball and hitting someone with the bat. The former requires absolute alertness by the batter to avoid being hit. The use of a batting helmet is increasing to avoid injuries to the head from a pitched ball. The latter requires the batter to develop the habit of dropping the bat rather than throwing it. Spectators and other players except the team on the field be kept at least twenty feet from home plate.

Can you hit eight out of ten pitched strikes? Ten out of ten? Fifteen out of fifteen?

PRACTICE

All practice, whether pursued individually or in a group, should be directed at achieving certain goals such as placement, power, level swing, stride, and concentration.

Individual

Bat Swinging   Assume proper stance and visualize the ball coming to various corners over the plate. Attempt to swing to hit the ball.

Swing the bat while looking at yourself in the mirror. Check stride, position of arms, and level of swing.

Batting Problems and Corrections

Problem	Causes	Corrections
No Power	Grip choked	Use medium or long grip.
	Hitting off rear foot	Shift weight forward as bat swings forward.
	No wrist snap	Uncock wrist as ball is contacted.
Missing ball	Swinging too late	Use choke grip.
	Swinging too early	Use medium or long grip.
	Lack of concentration	See bat hit the ball.
Ball hit too far to batter's side	Early swing	Long or medium grip.
	Forward foot moved backward	Shorten stance and step toward the pitch.
Ball hit too far to side away from batter	Late swing	Choke or medium grip.
	Forward foot moved toward plate	Lengthen stance and step toward the pitch.
Ball is popped up	Swinging upward	Level swing
Ball is hit into ground	Chopping downward	Level swing
Bunt goes too far	Right hand not giving	Relax right hand and recoil arms.
Bunt is popped up	Hitting high pitches	Hit only waist-high or lower pitches.
	Not pushing downward	Follow through downward.

Can you hit a line drive or a fly off a batting tee past the infield ten consecutive times? fifteen? Can you direct the ball between first and second base? What precautions must you take in executing each of the three basic slides to prevent your spikes from catching?

Swing two or three bats for a short period of time to build arm strength and thus increase the power of your swing.

Repeat the above exercises while employing bunting technique.

Batting Tee   Swing at a ball on a batting tee. If you cannot obtain one for practice, make one by attaching a ten-inch metal tube to a wooden base. Extend the tube to normal batting height by attaching a rubber radiator hose to it. The ball should be hit slightly ahead of the plate. See figure 4.15.

Adjust the tee position and adjust follow-through to practice place-hitting at various targets.

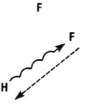

Figure 4.15   Batting Tee   Figure 4.16   Pepper Practice

Group

Group practice gives you the advantage of practicing under the watchful eye of an expert who can observe your mistakes and give you advice on how to overcome them.

Regular Pitcher   The best batting practice is against a regular pitcher. Practice swinging at balls pitched to certain target spots. Include concentrated placement, power, and bunting practice.

Pitching Machine   Adjust the machine to pitch the ball at various speeds and targets.

Pepper   Two hitters stand about fifteen to twenty feet in front of the group and practice hitting balls thrown or pitched by members of the group in rapid succession. Additional balls may be added. This practice is excellent for training the eyes to follow the ball. The ball should be chopped downward to hit the ball directly back to members of the group. See figure 4.16.

EVALUATION

A good way to evaluate batting is to utilize a checklist to determine accuracy of form, but more importantly, the best measure is your batting average. You can figure it by dividing the total number of hits you have made by the total number of times you have been at bat. A batting average of .300 or more is considered excellent.

In practice, can you successfully sacrifice bunt pitched balls six times in succession? Drag bunt? Push bunt? Can you direct your sacrifice bunts to the left and right of home plate?

BASERUNNING

Instructional Objectives

The learner will be able to—

1. run efficiently and swifty to first base and to other bases after becoming a base runner.
2. slide on close plays to avoid being tagged.

Softball games are often decided by one run. Alert, aggressive, intelligent baserunning often can make the difference between winning or losing. If you are playing on a team and have coaches at first and third bases, allow the coaches to assist you in determining your baserunning actions.

Running to First Base

(See figure 4.17.)

1. Push off on forward foot (left, for right-handed batters).
2. Step forward with right foot.
3. Run as fast as possible in a straight line.
4. Do not break stride to look at the ball unless it is behind you or you have no coach.
5. Run full speed over first base if a play is expected there, pull up as soon as possible in event of an overthrow to enable advancing.
6. Curve your run to round the bag if the play is away from first base.

Figure 4.17   Takeoff to First Base

Running to Bases Beyond First Base

1. Turn out to the right several feet before reaching first base by leaning to the right and taking a couple of steps at an angle away from the foul line.
2. Plan to touch the inside corner of the bag without slowing down as you change directions.
3. Touch the bag with either foot as you round the bag, but be prepared to stop if it seems unlikely that you will be able to make it to second base.
4. Straighten out run toward the next base.

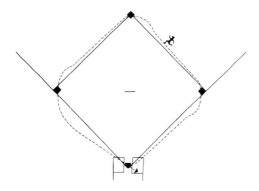

Figure 4.18   Rounding the Bases

5. Continue to curve out several feet before each base you intend to round.
6. Run straight to a base to which the play is to be made.
7. Touch the inside corner of the bag with your left foot and cross your right foot toward the next base. (See figure 4.18.)

Good baserunning requires speed and alertness. When you know that you can make a base easily, plan to round it so that you will be able to continue to the next base.

Sliding

A good base runner should slide on close plays except when running from home to first base. A slide has two advantages. First, it will stop your run without causing you to lose speed; second, it will give the infielder a small target to touch if it is a tag play. There are four basic types of slides: straight-in, bent-leg, head first, and hook. (See figs. 4.19, 4.20, and 4.21). When planning to slide, do not slow your speed during your approach to a base.

Figure 4.19   Touching the Base

Figure 4.20   Bent-leg Slide

Figure 4.21   Headfirst Slide

The *straight-in slide* starts about ten feet from the bag. Lean away from the base and lift up either leg while momentarily extending the other leg downward to the ground. This action will cause the bottom leg to skid along the ground. To prevent the spikes from catching, the skidding leg should immediately be bent at the knee and the extended leg lifted well off the ground. The arms do not come in contact with the ground.

The *bent-leg slide* is executed in order to stop your speed at a base but allows you to get back on your feet immediately to proceed to another base if pos-

Figure 4.22   Hook Slide

sible. Choose this slide if you are unsure about the accuracy of the throw or the closeness of the play. The bent-leg slide is like the straight-in slide except that it is started nearer the base and the backward fall is checked. The nonsliding leg is bent at the knee instead of extended. As soon as the skidding leg touches the base, the weight is brought forward by thrusting the arms forward, thus pulling the body up and shifting the weight to the top leg, which is bent and ready to brace your next running step with the unweighted sliding leg.

The *headfirst* slide has increased in popularity despite its potential for upper body injury because it provides an extremely small tag area. The slide begins about eight feet from the bag. Lean forward toward the base, extend the arms and catch your weight on the heels of the hands and chest. Keep your head up.

The *hook slide* is used to avoid a tag by the infielder. The sliding foot barely touches the corner of the bag away from the fielder, and the body falls away from the base. This action allows a very small part of the body to be touched by the ball. The takeoff for a hook slide may be with either foot. Again the weight is thrown backward, but both feet are bent sideways to prevent the spikes from catching. As the touching foot approaches the bag, the upper part of the body and the nonsliding leg are twisted away from the fielder. Once you make a decision to slide, never change your mind! If you change your mind, your spikes might catch the turf and could cause a leg injury.

The Leadoff

Once you have gained a base, you of course will want to reach the next base. Until the ball leaves the pitcher's hand, you must stay on your base. You may not lead off in slow-pitch softball. It is important, however, that you be ready to run. A good leadoff is essential for advancing to another base, either by stealing (fast-pitch only) or by advancing on a batted ball.

An effective stance is crucial to the success of a good leadoff. The left foot is placed on the inside edge of the base; the other foot may be placed either a step in front or a step behind the left foot. The latter method is used to get the body in motion before the ball leaves the pitcher's hand. A stride is taken as the pitcher's arm starts forward, but the runner must be careful not to leave the base before the ball is released. This stance should not be used in slow-pitch softball. Regardless of the method, the body faces the next base, knees are flexed, and the weight is on the forward foot. Arms are bent and held free of the body, ready to generate momentum. The runner takes two or three steps, stops, and returns if the ball is not hit. The body should be kept under control.

Can you perform a hook, bent leg, and head first slide? Do you know when to use each type?

Figure 4.23   Conventional Lead-off
Stance

Figure 4.24   Rolling-start Leadoff

Stealing

Study the pitcher and catcher and watch the infielders for weaknesses that may enhance the success of an attempted steal. It will help you to steal a base if the catcher has a weak throwing arm or tends to ignore your leadoff, or if the infielders seem to be slow to protect the base you seek. Regardless of these weaknesses, if a coach is not giving directions the following should be considered before attempting to steal:

1. Game score
2. Pitcher's ability
3. Number of outs
4. Ability of succeeding batters
5. Inning you are playing

If you plan to steal the next base, it is important that you do not reveal your intent before the ball leaves the pitcher's hand so that you will not alert the defensive team. As soon as the ball leaves the pitcher's hand, lower your body, accelerate with short, digging steps and lengthen to full stride until the base is reached. Be prepared to slide.

Delayed Steal   This is a risky play and should be attempted only by swift runners. Lead off the base as usual. If the catcher does not force you back, immediately take off at full speed for the next base as soon as he starts to throw the ball to the pitcher. This type of steal can be most effective if there are less than two outs and runners are on first and third bases. The runner on first runs about halfway to second and stops or slows down, deliberately tempting the catcher to throw. If the ball is thrown to second, the runner on third base breaks toward home at full speed. If the ball is not thrown to second, the first-base runner can take second base unchallenged.

Safety

Baserunning can be one of the most dangerous aspects of softball play. You should follow these suggestions:

1. Be aware of fielders and attempt to avoid collisions.
2. Contact the corner of the base away from the baseman whenever possible to avoid bumping him.
3. Never change your mind while in the act of sliding.
4. Avoid sliding without proper protection for your legs.
5. Slide to avoid contact with the baseman.

Baserunning Problems and Corrections

Problem	Causes	Corrections
Slow start from plate or base	Striding too far on the first step	Take short, digging steps.
	Not keeping weight low	Don't look at ball; keep head down.
Sliding too early	Misjudging beginning distance	Place markers to the side of sliding area for practice.
Sliding too late	Indecision	Plan to slide and do it.

PRACTICE

Individual

Actual Baserunning   Practice overrunning first base; then, making the turn; then, running to first and second bases; then running from first to third, and finally, running all the way. Carry a stopwatch. Try to improve your time.

Starts   Swing bat and take off to full stride. Repeat several times. Stand on base and take off to full stride.

Sliding   Slide on smooth surface indoors to a loose base; then, try grass; then, use a sand pit; and finally, slide on the dirt. Wear protective clothing.

Group

Baserunning   Run in pairs to the various bases. Time each player's run.

Stealing   Place base runner on first base. Have the pitcher pitch and have the catcher attempt to throw the runner out.

Starts   Base runner assumes leadoff stance, leaves on signal, stops on whistle, and returns.

EVALUATION

Develop a checklist to evaluate starts, leadoffs, and slides. Keep a record of the attempted steals, and divide the successful attempts into the total attempts to secure the percentage of successful attemps. Time each player's running speed to the various bases.

REFERENCES

Barnes, Mildred, et al. *Sports Activities for Girls and Women.* New York: Appleton-Century-Crofts, 1966.

Breen, James. "What Makes a Good Hitter?" *Journal of Health, Physical Education and Recreation* 38 (April 1967):23-25.

Dobie, Dottie. "Run Your Way to Victory," *1972-74 Softball Guide.* Washington, D.C.: Division for Girls and Women's Sports, American Association for Health, Physical Education and Recreation.

Dobson, Margaret, and Sisley, Becky. *Softball for Girls.* New York: Ronald Press, 1971, chapter 13.

Drysdale, Sharon J. "A Bunting Guide." *1979-81 Softball Guide.* Washington, D.C.: National Association for Girls and Women's Sports, American Alliance for Health, Physical Education and Recreation.

Joyce, Joan and Anquillare, John. *Winning Softball.* Chicago: Henry Regnery Company, 1975.

Marcotte, Joan. "Using the Batting Tee." *1979-81 Softball Guide.* Washington, D.C., National Association for Girls and Women's Sports, American Alliance for Health, Physical Education and Recreation.

Moore, Johnna. "Strategy of Baserunning." *Softball Reprint of Articles, 1969.* Washington, D.C.: Division for Girls and Women's Sports, American Association for Health, Physical Education and Recreation.

Neal, Patsy. *Coaching Methods for Women.* Reading, Mass.: Addison-Wesley, 1969.

REDDECK, GWEN. "What? When?—Bunt, Squeeze, Hit/Run." *Softball Reprint of Articles, 1969.* Washington, D.C.: Division for Girls and Women's Sports, American Association for Health, Physical Education and Recreation.

WALSH, LOREN. *Coaching Winning Softball.* Chicago: Contemporary Press, 1979.

Women's Softball. Mary Littlewood, consultant. Chicago: Athletic Institute, 1971.

defensive skills

5

The shortness of the base paths and the size of the ball give the offensive team an advantage. Consequently, good softball play requires good defensive play. Every player needs to possess skill in fielding ground balls, catching fly balls, and the ability to throw with speed and accuracy. In addition, knowledge of where to throw and when and how to protect a base is vital to good defensive playing ability.

FIELDING

Instructional Objectives

The learner will be able to—

1. field ground balls and throw out a runner,
2. catch fly balls in both the infield and outfield,
3. receive throws and tag out a runner,
4. plan ahead so that cutoff plays, backing up, and base covering are executed.

Catching fly balls, stopping balls hit on the ground, and catching throws are the basic skills needed for good fielding. In all cases there are common principles that govern the proper fielding of the ball.

Stance

Whenever you are in a defensive position, you must be alert and ready. Figure 5.1 illustrates the proper waiting or ready position.

1. Feet are comfortably spread.
2. Body faces batter, and eyes are fixed on ball.
3. Knees and hips are bent
4. Weight is on balls of both feet.
5. Keep the glove out in front, wide open and facing the batter.

Figure 5.1   Waiting Positions

While practicing, can you successfully field six grounders and throw the first two accurately to first base, the second two to second base, and the third two to third base?

Do you know what to do as a baseman to avoid collisions at the base with the base runner?

It is important that you stay relaxed throughout your fielding attempt. If the ball is hit or thrown softly, or shallow, or to the left or right, move diagonally toward it. Conversely, if it is hit or thrown sharply or deeply to the left or right, move diagonally backward. The speed of your movement depends on the exact speed of the ball and the distance it is from you.

Fly Balls

When a *fly ball* is hit, move at the crack of the bat in the direction of the ball. Run as fast as you can so that you can be there in time to wait for it, if at all possible. The speed, direction, height, and effect of the wind on the ball should be determined immediately, and a judgment should be made as to about where the ball can be caught. This judgment is made as you are already on the move to that spot. The sound of the bat against the ball, as well as the visual sighting of the speed of the ball, will give you some immediate information as to where to go. If the ball is hit high, you will have a little more time to get there than if the ball is hit low. Be prepared for final adjustments while waiting for the ball to descend if a high wind is blowing. If the ball is going to come down behind you, turn to whichever side is necessary, using whatever footwork comes naturally. Look over your shoulder at the ball as you move backward and sideways for it. Try to avoid having to turn your back on the ball. Be sure you are back far enough to catch the ball, because it is easier to take a step or two forward

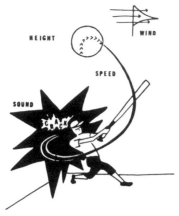

Figure 5.2   Judging a Fly Ball

Figure 5.3   One Hand Catch of Fly Ball

than it is to back up. As the ball descends, get ready for the ball by standing with your legs comfortably spread, with the leg opposite to the throwing arm slightly ahead so that you are ready to throw. Try to reach about head high for the ball to save time in making the catch; and when running for the ball, have your glove out ready to catch it. Always try to be prepared to return the ball quickly. When there are baserunners and if time permits, attempt to run or "loop" back a few steps behind where you plan to catch the ball so that you will be moving toward the base that you expect to be throwing to as you catch the ball. Improvements in gloves have increased the use of catching flyballs with one hand. Such a practice increases range and stability.

Try to catch every ball in your area unless by catching a foul you would allow a base runner to advance or score in a close game. As soon as you know you can catch the ball, warn your teammate by shouting, "I have it!" If you hear this signal from someone else before you call it, immediately move away from the ball to avoid collision with the teammate who is fielding the ball. Collisions may result in errors or serious injuries.

Figure 5.4   Moving Back to Catch a Fly Ball

Figure 5.5   Moving in to Catch a Fly Ball

Ground Balls

Ground balls seldom are affected by a wind factor, but the surface of the playing field often causes the ball to bounce erratically, which causes difficulty in judging where to catch it. Just as in fielding fly balls, the decision based on the sound of the crack of the bat against the ball and the speed and direction of the ball must be made immediately so that no time is wasted in getting in the proper place to stop the ground ball. Since the batter is not out on a ground ball until the ball reaches the base he is attempting to reach, move quickly toward the ball. Avoid letting the ball "play you" by not moving backward on it. Shift your weight forward, pivot toward the side the ball is coming from, and run in a low position to save time in bending down for the ball at the last second. Time your run so that you can catch the ball just after it starts its bounce. This timing will avoid erratic twists and will save time. As the ball nears you, stop running and brace yourself by spreading your feet comfortably.

There are five procedures that should be used for stopping ground balls. (Study fig. 5.4.)

1. Place your glove-hand foot forward.
2. Bend your knees and hips low so that your hands touch the ground when hanging relaxed.

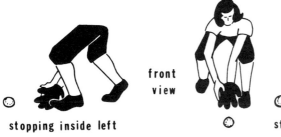

front
view

stopping inside left   stopping inside right

Figure 5.6   Fielding a Ground Ball

3. Move so that you are in line with the ground ball.
4. Stop the ball inside your glove-hand foot.
5. Watch the ball roll into the glove, and secure the ball with your throwing hand.

Always try to stop the ball with the glove-side foot forward and near the inside of that foot. This action allows better viewing of the ball and places the body in a good balanced position for throwing. If the ball is hit slowly, charge the ball by cutting diagonally to the right or left if necessary. If the ball is hit with great speed, move diagonally backward to the right or left. If there is not enough time to get the glove-side foot forward, try to block the ball with the body and/or field the ball off the non-glove foot. Occasionally a ground ball may bounce high, in which case the ball is taken about head high. Use two hands to field the ball if possible. Concentration, alertness and quickness are essential to good felding of ground balls.

Do you know what is meant by "looping" to catch a fly ball and when this technique should be tried?

Thrown Balls

The same ready position is assumed for catching *thrown balls* as is used for grounders or fly balls. However, the position should not be assumed until the last moment before the ball is to be caught. This avoids warning the approaching base runners of the closeness of the play.

First, wait for the ball in a position of readiness with the feet comfortably spread, weight evenly distributed on the balls of both feet and on the hips,

Waiting for Throw   Catching Action

Figure 5.7

Figure 5.8   Catching Position

below   waist   above   waist

with knees slightly bent. Never take your eyes off the ball. If the ball comes to you below your waist, put your little fingers together and point the fingers downward; if it comes to you above your waist, put the thumbs together and point your fingers upward. This hand action permits better arm freedom and eliminates the possibility of the ball's jamming the ends of your fingers. Next, as the ball enters the mitt or glove, allow your hands to retreat toward your body. This action is called "give" and deadens the speed of the ball so that it is less likely to bound out of the glove. Simultaneously with the "give," cover the ball with your throwing hand so that the ball is trapped inside the glove. Immediately begin to grip the ball for the throw (see fig. 5.6).

Covering the Base

If the catch is a force-out play, catch the ball, touch the base, and move immediately out of the way so that you are free to make another throw and are safe from being bumped by the runner.

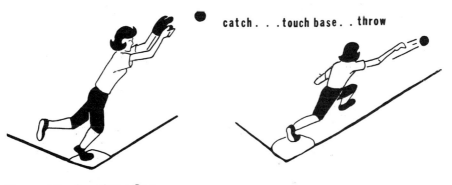

catch. . .touch base. . throw

Figure 5.9   Covering a Base

Tag Play

(Study figures 5.10 and 5.11.)
If the play is a tag play away from the base, make the tag and move away. The runner may be tagged with the ball in the glove. Avoid tagging a runner with the ball in your bare hand, where it can easily be jarred loose. For a tag play at

Figure 5.10 Tag at a Base

Figure 5.11 Tag for Upright Runner

Figure 5.12 Fielding and Throwing

a base, straddle the bag, and place your glove hand in front of the base, and let the runner slide into it. Keep yourself balanced, weight forward, so that you can avoid being "taken out of the play" by colliding with the oncoming base runner.

A fielder must be alert and ready to judge the ball accurately and quickly, to run rapidly and catch the ball surely, and to execute the throw immediately. Fielders must watch the ball until it is firmly resting inside their glove.

Safety

Keep several things in mind when playing defense to protect against injury

1. When waiting for a throw, keep your feet on the side of the base so they will not be stepped on.

2. When forcing out a base runner, touch the base with your foot and move quickly away to avoid a collision.
3. When fielding a fly ball or grounder where it is possible for more than one fielder to reach it, the player in the best position should call out his intentions.
4. Protect your throwing hand by fielding only with the "glove" hand.

Fielding Problems and Corrections

Problem	Causes	Corrections
Misjudging the ball	Not paying attention	Concentrate. Talk it up.
Late arriving	Not ready	Assume a ready stance.
	Poor start	Keep balanced.
Fumbling	Thinking about throwing	Concentrate first on catching the ball.
Bad hop on ball	Rough infield	Smooth out.
Dropping throws or flies	Not "giving"	Relax hands as ball reaches glove.

PRACTICE

Individual

Grounders   Stand several feet from a wall and throw the ball against it so that it will rebound off the wall to the floor or ground. Stop it in proper fielding position.

Fly balls or pop-ups   The ability to judge and catch pop-ups or fly balls can be improved by throwing a ball as high in the air as possible and then trying to catch it.

Group

Grounders   Throw or bat a grounder to each baseman, beginning with the third baseman, then the shortstop, and so on. Each fielder throws the ball to the first baseman, who throws it to the catcher. The catcher throws the ball back to first base, and the ball is then thrown to different basemen covering the bases.

Fly Balls   Throw or bat fly balls to each outfielder who then throws the ball on one bounce to the catcher or to a cutoff fielder, who relays the throw on command.

X X X X X X   X   X (Tosser)
                (Fielder)

Figure 5.13

DIRECTIONS FOR THE DOER:

Ask someone to check whether you are following the suggestions below while you field 5 ground balls, either hit or rolled directly to you from a distance of about 80 to 90 feet:

———————————— Knees bent when picking up the ball.

———————————— Eyes on the ball.

———————————— Glove foot in front of non-glove foot about shoulder width apart.

———————————— Ball field off the glove foot side.

———————————— Ball secured by the throwing hand.

OBSERVER:

Look at the points above. Watch the performer field 5 ground balls. Check the suggestions above that were followed.

Figure 5.14   Fielding Checklist

Reaction Footwork Drill   While facing a leader, the fielders move to positions on the field. On command they move forward, sideward, backward, utilizing proper pivoting and body positions for fielding.

Reaction Pickup   Form groups of four to six players. Each player takes a turn at being a tosser. Tossers throw grounders to the right, left, or directly at a player, forcing him forward or backward from a distance of about fifteen feet. Rotate after about ten tries.

EVALUATION

Fielding success may be evaluated by keeping a record of your fielding average (see fig. 5.14). It is computed by dividing your total putouts and assists by your total putouts, assists, and errors. A fielding average of .970 or better is considered excellent.

Fielding Grounders Test[1]

Use dimensions listed in figure 5.15.

Testee fields twenty grounders thrown by the tester every five seconds into the shaded area. Each throw must strike the ground before passing line A. The

---

1. David K. Brace, *Skills Test Manual: Softball for Girls* (Washington, D.C.: American Association for Health, Physical Education and Recreation, 1966), pp. 30-31.

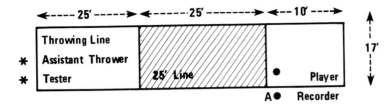

Figure 5.15   Grounder Test

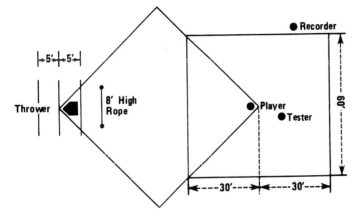

Figure 5.16   Fly Ball Test

testee fields ball cleanly, tosses it aside, and immediately attempts to field the next throw. Score one point for each successful pickup.

Take your usual defensive position on the field. Ask a batter to hit fly balls to you. Can you catch five in succession? Can you catch five in succession when you are required to run backwards for them?

Fly Ball Test[2]

Throw twenty fly balls to a fielder in a sixty-foot catching zone. The score is the number of balls caught out of two trials of ten throws each.

THROWING

Instructional Objectives

The learner will be able to—

1. throw the ball with sufficient distance and accuracy for his/her desired defensive position,

2. Brace, *Skills Test Manual: Softball for Boys* (Washington, D.C.: American Association for Health, Physical Education and Recreation, 1966), pp. 32-33.

2. throw the ball sidearm, if an infielder; overhand, if an outfielder; or with an overhand snap, if a catcher.

A good portion of defensive skill depends on the ability of the fielder to throw rapidly and accurately. No matter how well you can field a ball, if you cannot throw it properly the value of your fielding will be considerably reduced.

The Grip

The ball should be gripped in one of two ways. The method you select should suit the size of your hand. If your hands are large, hold the ball between your thumb and first two fingers, with your third and fourth fingers resting against the ball as far around the bottom of the ball as you can comfortably reach. If your hands are small, modify the grip so that the third and fourth fingers are spread around the side and bottom of the ball to provide better support. If possible, the fingers should cross the seams of the ball to prevent slipping when the ball is released. Only the finger pads should touch the ball. The finger pads have the best ability to feel the ball and allow maximum joint action for whipping the throw. Do not allow any other part of the hand or palm to touch it. You should be able to see daylight between your hand and the ball. Grip the ball firmly while it is still in your glove so you can quickly and surely remove it. The glove helps to support the ball as you position your fingers.

Basic Throws

There are five basic types of throws: the overhand, the overhand snap, the sidearm, the underhand toss, and the underhand pitch.

Throwing technique is basic to all throws. The major difference lies in the position of the hand and of the upper and lower arm in the forward thrust of the arm in the throw.

Overhand Throw   Only the arm position on the windup, or backswing, and the follow-through vary with the various types of throws. The basic throw for all players and the only throw used by outfielders, is the overhand throw. The advantage of the overhand throw is the speed and power that can be imparted to it. The disadvantage of the overhand throw is the extra time it takes. In using the overhand throw, raise the upper arm shoulder high, lift the forearm above the head, and flex the wrist so that your hand points behind you. Lift your upper arm overhead as you move the arm forward. Make your follow-

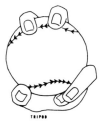 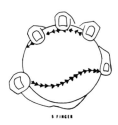 

Figure 5.17   Throwing Grips

through downward. These are the steps to follow to make a good overhand throw.

1. Grip ball firmly in the glove.
2. Shift weight to rear foot.
3. Move front foot a stride toward your target.
4. Swing throwing arm back behind your head, and cock wrist backward.
5. Whip the ball forward by shifting weight and body to the front foot to brace the action.
6. Pivot entire body so that you are nearly square with the target.
7. Move forearm forward when the elbow is above the shoulder.
8. Snap wrist just as the ball is to be released.
9. Continue entire body around in a free, natural follow-through.

A maximum backward stretch will develop power for your throw. The whipping action begins in the shoulder. When you release the ball, you will be off-balance unless you let your rear leg move forward to about shoulder distance from your supporting leg. If you stop the follow-through, you will lose power and accuracy, (2) unleash the power, and (3) follow through.

Figure 5.18   Throwing Action

Figure 5.19   Overhead Snap

For a long throw from the outfield, the ball is released a bit sooner than in the basic release in order to send it in a higher trajectory. The shorter the throw, the later it is released. If the throw is for a force-out play, aim it shoulder high at the receiver. If the throw is for a tag-out, it should be aimed at the base. If you must make a long throw, such as from the outfield to home plate, you can eliminate throwing the ball too high by planning to throw the ball so that it will land about ten feet in front of the receiver. The ball can then be caught on one bounce.

Overhand Snap   The overhand snap throw is used primarily by the catcher and occasionally by infielders when they don't have time for a full windup. The overhand snap is executed similarly to the overhand throw, except that the windup and follow-through are shortened in order to save time. The windup ends when the ball is brought about to the ear. A powerful wrist snap is important in order to gain the distance needed. The follow-through ends almost immediately after the ball is released.

Underhand Toss   The underhand toss is used on short throws which must be made quickly. The upper arm and forearm are both extended down in the backswing. The wrist extends so that the hand is pointing upward. On the forward swing, the arm comes forward with the upper arm extending downward; but as the ball is released, the upper arm extends forward. If you need to cover considerable distance, whip the forearm and wrist forcefully forward. The follow-through should be up and overhead.

Sidearm Throw   The sidearm throw is most often used by infielders to throw the ball when they are in a hurry. It is executed by extending the upper arm

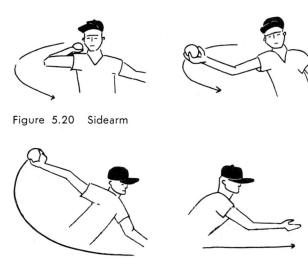

Figure 5.20   Sidearm

Figure 5.21   Underhand Pitch

diagonally out and down from the shoulder and extending the forearm directly up from the elbow. As the arm is brought forward, the upper arm maintains its relative position, but the forearm is dropped down so that it is parallel with the ground. When the ball is released, the arm continues around the body sideways.

Underhand Pitch   The under hand pitch is used to deliver the ball to the batter. The details of proper pitching technique are discussed in chapter 6.

ADVANCED DEFENSIVE SKILLS

The Preplan

Every defensive player should be thoroughly acquainted with the ability of the batter, the placement of the base runners, the placement of the defense, the score, the number of outs, and the count on the batter. Develop a plan of action for all the various possibilities for a play in your area. As the ball is pitched, be ready to move and be convinced that the play will be in your area. Never hesitate. Hesitation time can make the difference between an out and a hit.

Cutoff Throws

The purpose of a cutoff throw is to put out an advancing runner but at the last second to allow for changing the play if the throw promises to be unsuccessful. Cutoff throws from an outfielder are usually taken by the shortstop or first

Figure 5.22 Cutoff Throw

baseman. Occasionally the pitcher, second baseman, or a shortstop may cut off a catcher's throw to second base to stop a steal from first to second when there is also a runner on third base. In either case, the intervening fielder places himself in line with the throw, makes the final judgment on the possible success of the play, and decides whether to catch the throw and redirect it or to allow it to continue to its original destination. The decision to let the throw go through or to cut it off is made with the help of nearby noninvolved teammates who can assess the possible success of the throw. The fielder must throw the ball on a line so that it is not too high for the intervening fielder to catch.

Safety

Follow these procedures to protect against injury.

1. Warm up your arm before attempting difficult throws.
2. Throw the ball to basemen on the side opposite from where the base runner is expected.
3. The infielder should bend down to avoid being struck by a thrown ball intended for a player beyond him.

Throwing Problems and Corrections

Problem	Causes	Corrections
Ball misses target		
Right or high	Releasing ball too soon	Snap wrist. Hold off the release a bit longer.
	Off-balance	Stress shifting weight forward and pivot.
Left or low	Releasing too late	Let go of ball sooner.
Ball is short of target	Weak throwing arm	Change to less demanding position.
		Exercise throwing arm through weight training.

Figure 5.23   Throwing Practice

PRACTICE

Individual

Throw Against a Wall   Throw a ball against a target on the wall. The ball will rebound, and if you stand close enough, you will be able to catch it on the rebound.

Throwing to Bases   Throwing to bases can be practiced by standing near a corner of a large room and throwing the ball against one wall, catching it, and throwing it at the wall to your right or left.

Throwing from the Outfield   Stand in outfield position with several balls. Place a target in the infield, such as a tire or a cone, and attempt to hit it.

Group

Repeat practices suggested for fielding except that the quality of the throw should be stressed.

EVALUATION

There are several reliable and valid skills tests for throwing. Accuracy and distance are the variables most often measured.

Throw for Distance

From a six-foot approach area, take three tries at throwing for distance. Measure the best throw to the nearest foot.

Repeated Throwing

Throw the ball repeatedly against a wall from behind a line 15 feet from the wall. The ball must hit above a 7½-foot line. The score is the number of hits against the wall in thirty seconds. The best of six tries is counted.

REFERENCES

BRACE, DAVID K. *Skills Test Manual: Softball for Girls and Softball for Boys.* Washington, D.C.: American Association for Health, Physical Education, and Recreation, 1966.

DOBSON, MARGARET, and SISLEY, BECKY. *Softball for Girls.* New York: Ronald Press, 1971. Chapters 3 and 10.

NEAL, PATSY. *Coaching Methods for Women.* Reading, Mass.: Addison-Wesley, 1969.

WALSH, LOREN. *Coaching Winning Softball.* Chicago: Contemporary Press, 1979.

Women's Softball. Mary Littlewood, Consultant. Chicago, Ill.: Athletic Institute, 1971.

defensive position
play
6

Fielding and catching are the fundamental defensive measures. The defensive team prevents runs from scoring by using these skills; however, each position requires its special application. All softball players should understand the basic requirements of each position in order to work together as a team.

THE PITCHER

Instructional Objectives

The learner will be able to—

1. pitch with accuracy in fast- or slow-pitch softball and with considerable speed in fast-pitch softball to deter successful hitting.
2. field the ball and throw out the batter or other base runners.

The pitcher is crucial to success in fast pitch softball. The initiation of activity begins with the pitcher, and probably seventy-five percent of winning in fast pitch softball will depend upon pitching. Strength and stamina are important attributes for a pitcher. In addition, excellent physique, energy, alertness, wisdom, and courage are needed. The most important requirement in either fast or slow pitch play, however, is accuracy or control. The pitcher must have the ability to pitch the ball consistently over the plate and in the strike zone. In fast-pitch softball, the objective is to make it impossible for the batter to hit the ball. Thus speed and deception are needed on each pitch. In slow-pitch softball, however, only accuracy is required, since the objective is to get the batter out after he has hit the ball.

Rules Governing Pitching

Action	Fast Pitch	Slow Pitch
Delivery	Underhand	Same
Feet	Both feet in contact with pitching plate.	Only one foot must be on the plate.
Step	One step may be taken toward the batter as ball is delivered.	Same.
Speed	Any amount permitted.	Moderate speed with a perceptible arc, not over ten feet.
Strike Zone	Over the plate and between batter's armpits and the tops of his knees.	Over the plate and no higher than batter's shoulders or lower than his knees.
Windup	Only one motion toward the batter is legal.	Not mentioned.

Fast-pitch Pitching

Concentrated practice is necessary in order to develop and control the variety of pitches necessary. Most pitchers use a windmill or a slingshot type of delivery. Windups have two purposes: (1) to deceive the batter and (2) to obtain full power from your entire body to add force to the pitch. Develop the windup and delivery that suits you best. There is a variety of pitches: fastball, change of pace, drop, curves, and a rise, or upshoot, pitch. Start your pitch by standing with both feet touching the pitcher's plate. Place the throwing-side heel on the front edge of the plate and the toe of the other foot on the back edge. Your feet should be approximately twelve inches apart. Face the batter and hold the ball in both hands in front of the body.

Types of Deliveries

Slingshot   Start your backswing by moving both hands forward toward the batter until your arms are comfortably extended straight out in front about waist high. When this point is reached, bring your throwing arm down and back along the hip line and up behind the body as far as it can comfortably extend. At the top of the backswing, cock your wrist by extending as far back as possible. The upper arm and forearm are diagonally upward, and the body is rotated almost a quarter turn toward the pitching-arm side. Start the forward motion with your body rotating forward, the arm swung downward and forward, parallel with the lateral line of the body. Bring your body weight forward as you take a natural step toward the batter on the foot opposite the pitching arm.

Figure 6.1　Slingshot Pitch

When the extended arm is about even with the side of the body just before the ball is released, snap your wrist forward and roll the ball off your fingertips to add power and spin to the pitch. After the ball leaves your hand, the arm continues to follow through, up and overhead with the arm completely extended. The foot on the pitching-arm side is brought up next to the forward foot in a fairly wide stance with the knees and hips relaxed. This position permits maximum balance after release of the ball and also puts you in a ready fielding position. As you develop your speed and control, try to release your fast pitch so that it will "break" by curving, rising, or dropping. Do not attempt to toss or pull the arm, but rather swing the arm freely and powerfully on your delivery.

Windmill　　The *windmill delivery* makes a complete circle from straight up overhead to behind your body and then downward and out toward the batter.

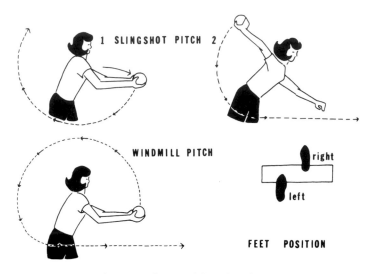

Figure 6.2   Pitching Windups and Foot Position

Start the delivery with both arms moving forward and upward, reaching out without stretching. Shift your weight to the foot on the pitching-arm side. As you take the ball from the glove, extend the upper arm diagonally outward from the shoulder and the forearm diagonally inward toward the body. As the hand reaches head-high, begin to lift the opposite foot off the rubber and forward in order to keep your balance. The arm is completely extended when it is dropped behind the body from head-high. You will gain momentum as you move into your downward swing. The nonpitching-side foot completes its step toward the plate in order to brace your body for the forward action and release of the ball. The pitching arm is thrust forward by pushing with the pitching-side foot against the rubber and then transferring this weight complete forward. Your follow-through is the same as for the slingshot delivery.

Note that the difference between these two deliveries is in the initial action of the pitching arm; that is, up, over, down, and forward for the windmill, and back, up, down, and forward for the slingshot delivery.

Types of Pitches

Once you have developed control and speed, you should learn other types of pitches. These pitches cause the ball to drop, to curve, to rise, and to change speeds in order to make it more difficult for the batter to hit the ball. Regardless of the type of pitch, the pitching action should be similar so that the batter does not know what kind of a pitch to expect.

For the *straight fast pitch* and the *slingshot delivery* grip the ball as for any other throw except that the hand is under the ball. Again, as for other throws, use either your entire hand or the tripod grip. Be sure your finger pads cross the seams of the ball.

A *curveball* makes the ball spin either toward or away from the batter. To pitch a curveball, grip the ball as for the fastball, but as it is released, snap the wrist to the left or to the right to cause the ball to roll off the inside or outside of the hand. The direction of snap depends on the direction you wish the ball to curve. Snap the wrist to the left to make the ball curve left and to the right to make it curve right. The *drop, of course,* makes the ball curve or break sharply downward. Use the same grip and delivery as for the fastball, but at the instant of the release, lift your thumb off the ball first, and then snap your first two fingers sharply upward. This action gives the ball more forward spin so that it will curve downward, or drop.

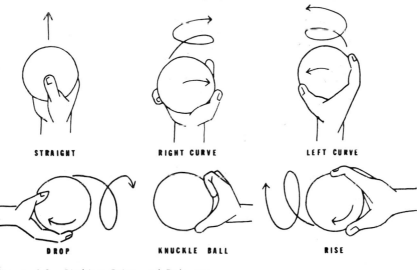

STRAIGHT   RIGHT CURVE   LEFT CURVE

DROP   KNUCKLE BALL   RISE

Figure 6.3   Pitching Grips and Releases

Using a wall target, can you pitch a straight fastball to each corner of the strike zone with 75 percent accuracy? A slow pitch?

The grip for the *rise* or *upshoot pitch* differs in that the ball is held with the fingers on top of the ball with the thumb underneath. As you release the ball, the wrist is extended or snapped upward, and the thumb pushes forward against the ball. This action imparts a backspin which should make the ball rise as it nears home plate. The effectiveness of these pitches will increase as you learn to add speed to the pitch. The *change-of-pace pitch* slows down the pitch and tends to throw off the timing of the batter. There are many grips for the change-of-pace pitch. The ball may be held in the palm of the hand with the fingers held loosely on the ball. It may be held by the knuckles or by digging your fingernails into it. Your pitching motion is again the same, but at the release the hand is opened with a snap of all four fingers, and the thumb merely extends forward. The ball must be released with equal pressure all around the ball so that no spin is imparted to it. The absence of spin will cause the ball to float or sail toward the batter. Controlling these various pitches and the development of speed will give you what is called "stuff." Concentrate first on pitching with as much speed and spin as you can accurately control.

Slow-pitch Pitching

Since the ball must travel through an arc of at least three feet, many pitchers will try to control the ball so that it reaches the maximum height close to the batter. The ball will descend as it crosses the plate and will be even with his or her back shoulder. This type of pitch often results in a pop-up. The slow-pitch pitcher should try to pitch to the desired corners of the plate and vary the height of the arc of the pitched ball. It is legal and desirable to place spins on the ball: forward, backward, or sideward.

Since only one foot must be in contact with the pitching plate be sure that the supporting foot is on the front edge of the plate so that when your stride is taken, your body can be as close to the target as possible at the instant of release.

Fielding Responsibilities

It is important that you as the pitcher are able to field your position. All balls hit toward you or bunted along the base lines are your responsibility. If the ball is hit too far to the left, allow the first baseman to field the ball as you proceed to cover first base. The pitcher backs up home plate on outfield hits with runners on base, and covers home plate when the catcher fails to catch a pitched ball. In addition, the pitcher backs up throws to third base.

Safety

Pitching is demanding, and it can be a dangerous position.

1. Be alert and balanced after delivering the ball to avoid being hit by sharply batted balls.
2. Be sure that the pitching plate and soil around the pitching area are firm to prevent slipping.

PRACTICE

Individual

Mimetic Pitching For about ten minutes daily practice your pitching form without using a ball. Assume stance, concentration, and take your windup, delivery, and follow-through.

Pitching Problems and Corrections

Problem	Causes	Corrections
Ball too high or far from batter	Release too late or stride too short	Release sooner. Practice consistent striding by marking desired spot.
Ball too low or close to batter	Release too soon or stride too long	Release later. Practice consistent stride.
Insufficient speed	Incorrect delivery action	Increase leverage by rotating spine and hip on throwing side away from batter. Stride as arm moves forward. Move arm forward as fast as possible. Snap the wrist on release.
Loss of balance	Incorrect stride and weight shift	Practice stride. Bring pitching-side foot up parallel with supporting foot after release of the ball.
	Incorrect stance	Feet shoulder-width apart.

Target Practice   Construct the strike zone on the wall. Take a basket of balls and pitch to planned areas on the target.

Speed   Increase speed as accuracy develops. Both should be practiced together. Try to pitch as fast as possible with accuracy.

Leg Strength   Run several times around the field daily to increase leg strength and overall physical endurance.

Group

Batting Practice   Pitch batting practice as a means of becoming accustomed to the individual batter's position and relation to the strike zone.

Observed Practice   Have someone with a checklist of the essential pitching fundamentals check our adherence to them.

EVALUATION

Win-Loss Record   Compile the total wins and losses.

Earned Run Record   Compute the Earned Run Average (ERA) by adding all earned runs scored against the pitcher as result of base runners getting on base other than by errors and by adding all the innings pitched. Multiply the earned runs by seven and divide by the innings pitched. The formula is:

$$\frac{ER \ (Earned \ Runs) \times 7 \ (innings \ in \ a \ game)}{IP \ (Total \ innings \ Pitched)}$$

Accuracy Test   Place a target on the wall as per figure 6.4. Fifteen legal pitches are permitted. Pitched balls striking within or on the line marking the inner rectangle count two points. Balls hitting the outer rectangle count one point. The score is the sum of points made.

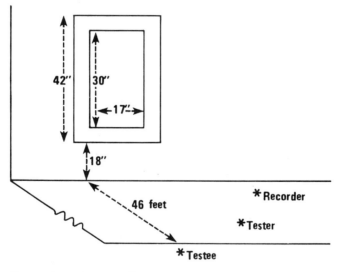

Figure 6.4   Accuracy Test

THE CATCHER

Instructional Objectives

The learner will be able to—

1. catch the balls thrown by the pitcher,
2. give reliable and accurate targets for the pitcher,
3. decide the pitch needed and signal the pitcher,
4. field the ball and throw out base runners,
5. direct the infield on where the play should be made on a bunt.

The catcher is the sparkplug of the team. He not only catches the pitches but also is in the best position to direct team defensive play. The catcher should be agile, alert, strong in the legs, and able to react quickly. He should be a natural leader with a competitive spirit and the ability to think quickly, decisively, and logically. A strong throwing arm is essential. The catcher is responsible for giving the pitcher advice on the type of pitch and the target for the pitch, catching pop-ups, throwing out runners attempting to steal, fielding bunts, protecting home plate, and backing up play at first or third base. The rules require that the catcher be in the catcher's box to receive the pitch, not interfere with the batter's attempt to swing at the ball, and wear a mask to protect the face. Women catchers must wear a chest protector.

Stance

The signal and the target for the pitch are given by the catcher when in a squat position. The squat position is assumed by bending the hips, knees, and ankles so that the body is as low as possible without resting the buttock on the ankles or the ground. Weight is on the toes, and knees are comfortably spread outward. At this point catchers choose one of two stances. Some continue to "sit down," whereas others "stand up," as illustrated in figures 6.5 and 6.6. The sit-down catcher stays on his haunches for the target. As the ball is pitched, the catcher rises on his toes into a crouch and thus is ready to meet the pitch, pivot, throw, or field. The stand-up catcher's stance is a bit more popular. He stands with knees bent and legs wide apart with the left foot ahead of the right. If the catcher is tall, this position is awkward and requires a great deal of bending.

Figure 6.5   Catcher Stand-up Stance

Figure 6.6   Catcher Sit-down Stance

Signals

The catcher and pitcher should agree on signals for the pitch. The catcher gives signals by extending the fingers of the throwing hand against the inside of his thigh when down in a squat position. Effort must be made to hide the signal from the offensive team. The pitcher has the prerogative of refusing the signaled pitch if he doesn't agree with it.

Target

After the signal is accepted, give the pitcher the target for the pitch by holding your mitt at the desired spot. As you hold your mitt up for the target clench the throwing hand in a loose fist to protect the fingers from the ball. Continue to hold the mitt on the target as the pitcher starts to pitch. When the ball leaves the pitcher's hand move up to a semistanding position with your feet spread diagonally outward approximately three feet apart. The change of position allows greater freedom of movement to catch the ball, to field it, or to throw out a runner. If the pitch should come low into the dirt, drop your left leg down parallel with the ground to block the ball. When the ball reaches your glove or mitt, absorb the force of the pitch by "relaxing" your arms into your waist.

Avoid giving a target in the middle of the strike zone. Keep the target steady until the ball leaves the pitcher's hand. The pitcher and catcher should study the batter and organize a strategy. The pitcher should throw balls that the batter finds difficult to hit. The ball should be pitched over the inside corner of the plate to batters who stand close to the plate, and over the outside corner of the plate to batters who stand far away from the plate. If the batter crouches, pitch the ball high. If he stands erect, pitch low balls. Change the pace of your delivery to power hitters and pitch fastballs to weak hitters. If the batter strides toward the pitch as he swings, pitch the ball inside. If the stride

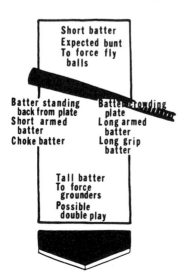

Figure 6.7   Pitching Area for Strike Zones

is away, aim your pitch to the outside corner of the plate. When the batter takes a long stride into the pitch, pitch high balls; conversely, if he takes a short stride pitch low balls.

The catcher must adjust his target and the type of pitch when there are base runners. With less than two outs and runners on base, the pitcher should pitch low and inside to force the batter to hit the ball into the ground for a double play or to prevent the batter from hitting the ball behind the runner on a hit-and-run play. If a bunt is expected, the pitch should be kept high because these pitches are often popped up.

Pitching patterns depend on the pitcher's control. Every pitcher must aim at a target, however, and the target should be a most effective one for that batter at that particular time and in that particular situation.

Throwing

The preparation for throwing must be accomplished quickly. The catcher uses a snap throw to the pitcher and, if strong enough, a snap throw to throw out runners attempting to steal and to field a bunt. With runners on base, the catcher should constantly try to reduce their leadoff by walking out in front of the plate and threatening to throw to the base or by simply walking them back to base. An occasional snap throw to the base may catch a base runner too far off to get back safely.

A snap throw begins from behind the ear and is thrown overhand with a snap of the wrist. The feet must be shuffled from the squat or stand-up stance so that the nonthrowing-side hip and foot are moving toward the intended target. Do not straighten up completely nor move in front of the plate. The throw should be free of spin and aimed at the fielder's knees on the side of the anticipated play. Do not wait for the infielder to cover the base.

Fielding

Immediately flip off your mask when you must field the ball or back up a play. Be alert and ready when a bunting situation is possible. Move with the batter, stay low, and pick up the ball with your throwing hand. Protect home plate on close plays by blocking it with your leg or body. Base runners will attempt to jar the ball loose from you so stay low and hold the ball with both hands. Back

Note the position of the batter's feet in relation to home plate. Where should the ball be pitched? Why?

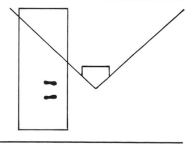

up all plays to first base when there are not runners on base. Since you face the entire defense, you serve as the defensive leader. The catcher calls out who is to field bunts, pop-ups, and short fly balls. Team spirit and hustle are encouraged and maintained by your example. If the pitcher gets upset, develops some flaw in his pitch, or begins to pitch too fast, the catcher should walk out to him, talk with him, encourage him, and in general try to settle him down.

INFIELDERS

Instructional Objectives

The learner will be able to—

1. catch balls thrown by teammates to put out base runners,
2. field batted and thrown balls,
3. cover and back up assigned bases.

Playing the infield requires specific physical ability and skill for each position. However, all infielders, including the pitcher and the catcher, must constantly be aware of the immediate situation such as (1) number of outs, (2) count on the batter, and (3) position of the base runners. With this information, you must think through what action you will need to take to play your position before each pitch. This process is fostered through constant communication with other infielders.

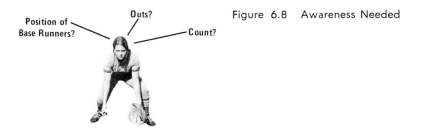

Position of Base Runners? Outs? Count?

Figure 6.8   Awareness Needed

First Baseman

The first baseman is involved in almost every play. Agility and height are helpful physical attributes for this position. Throwing to other bases is easier for left-handed players. The first baseman plays about six feet toward second base and two or three steps in front of the base, or more if the batter is fast or a sacrifice is in order to protect against a bunt. When two strikes have been called, he can move back four or five steps since a bunt is less likely. He receives all kinds of throws. Nimble footwork is essential. To cover the base for a putout, the first baseman stands in the usual ready position, facing the throw. If the ball comes straight to him, he steps toward the ball with the foot on his mitt side and touches the bag with the opposite foot. He reaches for the ball to save time. If the ball comes wide of the mitt side, he steps to that side, and touches

Figure 6.9   First Baseman Put-out Position

the bag with the same foot as for the straight-in throw. If the ball comes wide to the non-mitt side, he reaches across with his mitt to catch it and touches the base with his foot opposite the mitt side. On a pick-off play when the catcher throws the ball to try to put out the runner, if time permits, he straddles the bag with his feet facing second base and rotates the upper part of his body toward the throw. When he catches the ball, he swings his mitt down on the bag.

Second Baseman

The second baseman plays about fifteen feet toward first base from second base and about ten feet behind the base line. His job is to catch any fly balls or field any grounders in his territory. Since most of the second baseman's throws will go to first base or to the shortstop covering second base, a strong throwing arm is not necessary. However, agility in covering the base and ability to throw the ball quickly aids the second baseman in making double plays. When he is the middleman for a double play at second base, he times his run so that he will catch the ball as he steps on the base with his left foot. After catching the ball,

Figure 6.10   Double Play with Second Baseman

Figure 6.11   Force-out and Relay Throw

he takes one more step with his right foot to leave the base, then pivots on the right foot, and steps forward with his left foot as he throws to first base. The second baseman must be alert to receive throws from the catcher on attempted steals and on bunt plays to cover first base.

Shortstop

This very demanding position requires agility, speed, and a good throwing arm. The shortstop plays about halfway between third and second base and about ten to twelve feet behind the base line. As a shortstop you must be quick, agile, able to throw off-balance, and to run rapidly. When you are the pivot man on a double play, you usually run directly to the base, tag it with your left foot as you catch the ball, take one more step with the right foot, and throw to first base as you take your next step with the left foot. You will cover second base when the ball is hit to the right side of the infield and third base when the third baseman is fielding the ball.

Can you throw accurately sidearm from first to third base or third to first base five times in succession?

Third Baseman

Third base is called the "hot corner" because most batters are right-handed and tend to "pull" their hits toward third base. Therefore, as a third baseman, you must be able to field and throw in a rapid, smooth sequence. The third baseman plays about two to seven feet from the base and two or three steps in front of the base when there are less than two strikes on the batter. When a bunt is less likely, he moves back four or five steps. His job is to field all balls hit in this area and to cover third base on put-out plays.

Backing Up Bases   Every defensive player has a responsibility to back up plays in his area. The purpose of backing up is to prevent the taking of an additional base because of an error. The catcher usually backs up first base if there is no one on base. The pitcher usually backs up third base or home plate and, occasionally, first base. The first baseman occasionally backs up home

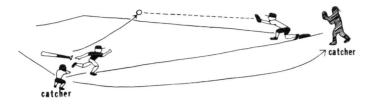

Figure 6.12   Backing Up Bases

Figure 6.13   Trapping a Runner

plate and second base. The shortstop backs up plays at third and at second base, and the third baseman backs up plays at second base on some outfield throws. The outfielders usually back up any batted or thrown ball to the infield that is in front of their areas and any batted ball to their immediate neighboring outfielder.

Covering   Each baseman is responsible for protecting his base. Be ready at all times to catch a throw to your base to put out a runner. However, occasionally you will be forced to field a ball while another runner is advancing to your base. In this case, the nearest available defensive player should be prepared to run to your base and take the thrown ball to put out the runner. If the catcher has moved from the plate to catch a pop fly, the pitcher moves to cover home plate if there is a runner on third base. The second baseman covers first base if the first baseman is forced to field a batted ball. In this situation, the shortstop automatically moves to second base to cover the base. If the shortstop is fielding a ball and a play is to be made to second base the second baseman covers the base. If the third baseman is fielding the ball, the shortstop will cover third base. These covering maneuvers can often be anticipated, but when they cannot, an advanced player moves instinctively to protect the base near him.

Trapping a Runner   When a base runner is caught between two bases, he is referred to as being trapped. In this situation defensive players close in on the runner from either side, throwing the ball to the player toward whom the runner is moving. In the meantime, other players back up the throw to protect against an overthrown ball or to tag out the runner if he should elude the trap. It is a good technique to fake a throw and then move toward the runner with the ball. If the tag cannot be affected, at least chase the runner back to the base from which he came.

Safety

Several procedures can help to guard against injury to infielders.

1. Be sure that home plate is secure and the area around it smooth and level.
2. Be sure that the infield is free of rocks, holes, and other obstructions.
3. Bases should be secured to the ground.
4. Catchers must keep the throwing hand clenched until the ball is caught and be alert to the danger of the swing at the ball and the throwing of the bat.
5. Call out your intentions to catch a pop-up.

Infielding Problem and Corrections

Problem	Causes	Corrections
Throw too late for a putout	Not charging the ball	Come to meet the ball.
	Taking too long to release the ball	Practice throwing from a semistanding position.
	Weak arm	Play a position needing less arm strength.
Failure to cover the base	Not thinking ahead	Infielders must communicate.
Failure to back up a play	Lack of concentration	Practice and reminders.

PRACTICE

Individual

Mimetic Footwork   Assume ready fielding position and practice moving forward, backward, and sideward to field the ball and then to move over to the base to cover.

Pivot and Throw   Place a base about ten feet from a wall. Position yourself the usual playing distance from the base. Place a ball on the floor at that point; then, pick it up, run to the base, and throw the ball against the wall.

Pop-ups   Throw a ball vertically at differing heights. Practice trying to catch the ball.

Group

Infield Practice   Throw or hit the ball from the batter's position to each infielder. The infielder fields the ball and throws to first base. The ball is then thrown to the catcher, catcher to third baseman, to second baseman, to first baseman, and then back to the catcher. The catcher flips the ball to the hitter or thrower who repeats the action to each infielder. The initial throw after fielding the ball may be made to other bases.

Trapping the Runners   Place a base runner between two infielders. The base runner attempts to return or advance to a base before being put out. Fielders practice throwing the ball and chasing the runner to make the putout. Add the various backup and covering assignments of the remaining infielders.

Double Play   Place a runner on first base and a base runner at home plate. A ball is thrown or batted to an infielder, who attempts to complete the double play. (Sliding can be practiced by the runner approaching second base.)

Can you describe several safety precautions that should be taken to avoid injuries in throwing or catching balls?

EVALUATION

Fielding Record   Keep a record of the attempted putouts and assists and the successful putouts and assists. To determine an average, divide the number of successes by the number of attempts.

$$\frac{\text{Successes}}{\text{Attempts}} = \text{Average of Fielding Success}$$

Rating Chart   Ask an observer to evaluate your fielding performance on the chart on page 68.

OUTFIELDERS

Instructional Objectives

The learner will be able to—

1. catch a fly ball hit into his assigned area,
2. throw the ball to the proper infielder to force out or to contain the actions of the base runner.
3. field ground balls,
4. back up other outfielders making a play.

An outfielder must be a good runner and possess a strong throwing arm. The distance in or out that an outfielder plays depends on several factors: the wind, the batter's ability, the score, the inning, and the location of base runners. In addition, the basic position is varied by moving to your right for left-handed hitters and to your left for right-handed hitters. The movement is increased in either direction for pull hitters.

An outfielder must learn to judge the ball immediately, run rapidly to catch the ball, and return the throw as quickly as possible. In addition to field-

Defensive Evaluation		
Name _____ Position		
Key: 5 = Excellent, 4 = Very Good, 3 = Average, 2 = Fair, 1 = Poor		
Item	**Rating**	**Comments**
1. Ready position	5 4 3 2 1	
2. Fielding position	5 4 3 2 1	
3. Throwing	5 4 3 2 1	
4. Covering	5 4 3 2 1	
5. Tagging	5 4 3 2 1	
6. Backing bases	5 4 3 2 1	

Figure 6.14

ing the ball, outfielders back up plays at the various bases in their areas, as well as for the outfielders nearest to them. Outfielders must be aware of base runners as well as the number of outs. The outfielder must decide as the ball is caught whether he can throw out a base runner. If a putout is possible, he will throw the ball on a line directly to the base. If he cannot throw that far on a direct line, he will throw the ball so that it will land a few feet in front of the base and hop into the infielder's glove. If it is not possible to gain a putout, he will return the ball one base ahead of the runner closest to home plate. Making unnecessary throws is always avoided. When the ball is hit deep and the throw is too long to reach its destination on one hop, he will throw to the second baseman or shortstop, who will relay the throw. The glare of the sun or field lights can sometimes hamper the vision of outfielders. Outfielders wear sunglasses, burnt cork, or shield their eyes from glare. It is the outfielder's responsibility to be aware of the wind direction and velocity, as well as the usual habits of the batter, and to adjust his position in the outfield accordingly. Short fly balls falling between the infield and outfield are usually the responsibility of the outfielders, since it is easier to move forward than backward. Outfielders must call out their intentions on these plays. It is imperative that outfielders communicate to each other whenever the ball is hit in areas that overlap.

Can you throw five overhead throws from left field to home plate with one bounce? Without a bounce?

Figure 6.15   Relay Throw

Center Fielder

The center fielder plays behind second base and is the fastest and most aggressive player in the outfield. As the center fielder, you are the leader of the outfield. Priority is given to you to field all balls to either the left or right. It is your responsibility to direct the proper playing positions of the other outfielders. The center fielder directs where the throw is to be made from the outfield. You will back up the other outfielders and the second baseman. When the ball is hit between two outfielders, the center fielder cuts over for the ball, and the other outfielders cut behind him to back up the play as noted in figure 6.15.

Left Fielder

The left fielder plays in the outfield between the third baseman and the shortstop. He backs up the center fielder and the third baseman when necessary. Usually the left fielder will play a bit closer to the foul line for right-handed hitters and a bit closer to center field for left-handed hitters. In addition, the left fielder backs up all throws made from the right side of the field.

Right Fielder

The right fielder plays between first and second base. He backs up the center fielder and the first baseman when necessary. Usually the right fielder plays a bit closer to the foul line for left-handed pull hitters and closer to the center fielder for right-handed pull hitters. In addition the right fielder backs up all plays made from the left side of the field.

Short Fielder

The short fielder is the tenth player permitted in slow-pitch softball. He may play as an extra infielder or outfielder or as a roving player. The exact position is determined by the team preference and/or situation. If the batter is a long-ball hitter, the short fielder may play as an outfielder; if the batter is an excellent place-hitter, then he may play as an extra infielder. As a rover, the short fielder plays between the infield and outfield, swinging more to the left for right-handed hitters and more to the right for left-handed hitters. The short fielder must be very versatile to be able to fulfill these roles. Speed, agility, and a good throwing arm are essential abilities.

No matter what your defensive roles, your ability to throw, to catch, to run, to judge the ball, and to think ahead will determine your true effectiveness.

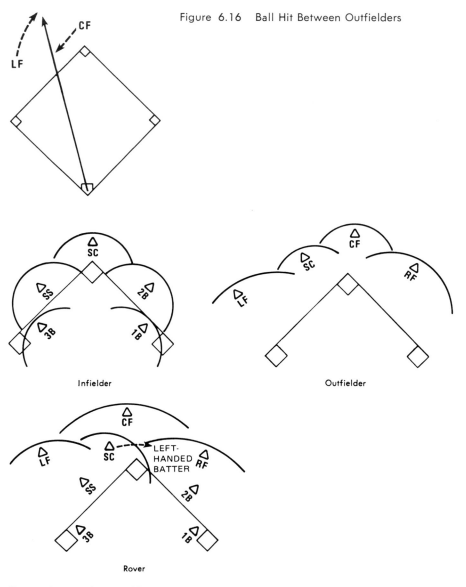

Figure 6.16   Ball Hit Between Outfielders

Infielder

Outfielder

Rover

Figure 6.17   Short Fielder Positions (Slow Pitch)

Safety

Outfielders should take the following precautions:

1. Call for the ball to avoid collisions with other fielders.
2. Know at all times where the fences are located. They should be padded for your protection.

Outfielder Problems and Corrections

Problem	Causes	Corrections
Slow start on the ball	Not paying attention	Concentration and communication from teammates.
Incorrect placement of throw	Poor judgment	Communication from center fielder.

PRACTICE

Individual

Fly Balls Throw golf balls to yourself at various angles and practice catching them.

Throwing Take a basket of softballs and practice throwing to the various bases as targets. Practice cutoff throws by placing a seven- to eight-foot marker near the infield and attempting to throw just above it.

Group

Ground Balls Ground balls are hit to the various outfielders who field the ball and throw to the catcher.

Fly Balls Same as above.

Throwing to Bases All types of hits are made to the outfielders, who are directed to throw the ball to the various bases.

REFERENCES

BATEWOOD, J., and DUMER, K. "Catcher Up." *1969 Edition of Softball Selected Articles.* Washington, D.C.: American Association for Health, Physical Education and Recreation.

BRACE, D. *Skills Test Manual: Softball for Girls and Softball for Boys.* Washington, D.C.: American Association for Health, Physical Education and Recreation, 1966.

DOBSON, MARGARET, and SISLEY, BECKY. *Softball for Girls*. New York: Ronald Press, 1971. Chapters 4-11.

GARDNER, F. "Tips for the Beginning Pitcher." *1972-74 DGWS Softball Guide*. Washington, D.C.: American Association for Health, Physical Education and Recreation.

HARRISON, PAT. "Thinking and Playing the Outfield." *1972-74 DGWS Softball Guide*. Washington, D.C.: American Association for Health, Physical Education and Recreation.

HUTCHINSON, JILL. "It's Catching." *1972-74 DGWS Softball Guide*. Washington, D.C.: American Association for Health, Physical Education and Recreation.

JOYCE, JOAN and JOHN ANQUILLARE. *Winning Softball*. Chicago: Henry Regnery Company, 1975.

KILLAIN, PAT. "Speed vs. Accuracy in Teaching the Softball Pitcher." *1979-81 NAGSW Softball Guide*. Washington, D.C.: National Association for Girls' and Women's Sports, American Alliance for Helth, Physical Education and Recreation.

KRAMER, BETTY. "The Cutoff Play and the Relay." *1979-81 NAGSW Softball Guide*. Washington, D.C.: National Association for Girls' and Women's Sports, American Alliance for Health, Physical Education and Recreation.

LOPIANO, DONNA. "Developing the Exceptional Slingshot Pitcher." *1974-76 Softball Guide*. Washington, D.C.: American Association for Health Physical Education and Recreation.

RICKER, MARGE. "The Run-Down Play." *1979-81 NAGSW Softball Guide*. Washington, D.C.: National Association for Girls' and Women's Sports, American Alliance for Health, Physical Education and Recreation.

SCHUNK, CAROL. "Tenth Man Theme." *1972-74 DGWS Softball Guide*, Washington, D.C.: American Association for Health, Physical Education and Recreation.

WALSH, LOREN. *Coaching Winning Softball*. Chicago: Contemporary Press, 1979.

WILSON, JAMIE. "Tips on Infielding." *1972-74 DGWS Softball Guide*, Washington, D.C.: American Association for Health, Physical Education and Recreation.

Women's Softball. Mary Littlewood, consultant. Chicago: Athletic Institute, 1971.

patterns of play
7

As your skill in the various softball techniques improves, so should your ability to execute these skills in planned offensive and defensive patterns. Your ability to score runs will increase when you are able to take advantage of circumstances that are conducive to getting a base hit or advancing to the next base. You should know how to adjust your position defensively to protect against offensive patterns that could result in the scoring of runs. If you are the pitcher, know the strategy as well as the techniques of pitching.

Instructional Objectives

The learner will be able to—

1. take advantage of prevailing defensive conditions to enhance opportunities to score runs,
2. take advantage of prevailing offensive conditions to prevent runs from being scored.

OFFENSIVE PATTERNS

Batting

When batting, your foremost thought should be to get on base. This goal will be achieved most often by getting a base hit. However, an assessment of the prevailing offensive and defensive situations should guide you in deciding on any adjustments in your batting plan. Shortening your grip on the bat so that you can swing the bat faster and more accurately will help you to hit a fastball pitcher or a pitcher with a great deal of "stuff." When the pitcher seems to lack control or seems to be getting tired, try to be very selective in swinging at pitches. It is advisable not to swing at a 3-0 pitch or even a 3-1 pitch, since a walk is likely. However, if you are a power hitter, your could possibly hit a "grooved pitch" (one in the center of the strike zone) for extra bases. As the batter, you have the advantage on a 3-2 pitch since you know that the pitcher must throw the next ball in the strike zone.

Surprise the defense with a bunt if they are playing back. Conversely, if they are playing in for a bunt, it might be wise to try to punch the ball over their heads. Swing at a pitch, but with no intention of hitting it when you know a base runner is going to steal. The swinging action confuses the catcher and often may cause him to make a poor throw. The usual offensive pattern in a close game is to try to get a runner on base, sacrifice him to second with a bunt, or have him try to steal second base so that a base hit can score him.

Batting Order

The order in which players are assigned to bat should be carefully determined. The first batter is often the shortest and fastest player on the team. He is a player who frequently gets on base. The second batter should be a good bunter or hit-and-run hitter. He should be able to advance the leadoff batter. The third, fourth, and fifth batters should be the most consistent and powerful hitters on the team. Their job is to bring home the earlier batters by hitting homers or extra-base hits. The weaker hitters follow. Usually the pitcher bats last.

The offensive team is permitted the option of using a "designated hitter" in fast pitch play only. A "designated hitter" becomes the tenth player in the lineup although he or she may bat in any position so indicated at the start of the game and on the lineup sheet. A designated hitter may not enter the game on defense and should be an outstanding hitter.

Baserunning

At the crack of the bat, have one goal in mind—to get on base. Be alert and take advantage of any misplay to reach the farthest base. When you know you can reach first base safely, immediately round the base and look for the ball and the position of the fielders. If an error occurs, or if you realize that a defensive player cannot cover the base you are attempting to reach, continue running.

Substitute Players

Substitute or "pinch" hitters are used when a crucial scoring opportunity is at hand and a better hitter, bunter, or a more powerful hitter than the scheduled batter is available and needed. A pinch runner is used if the run is needed and the base runner is slow. The base runner is removed from the game, and a speedier runner is substituted. In fast pitch and slow pitch play, any of the starting players except the "DH" in fast pitch may be withdrawn and re-enter once, provided such player occupies the same batting position, whenever he or she is in the lineup. However, a pitcher who is withdrawn cannot return to the pitching position for the remainder of the game.

As a batter in a game situation, do you remember to plan the desired placement of each hit prior to the pitcher's delivery? Keep a record of the number of hits you succeed in placing as planned.

DEFENSIVE PATTERNS

Fielding

Pitching is often considered the only defense a team has in softball. It is true that effective pitching will prevent base hits, but many base hits are gained simply because the fielders were not in proper position to protect their areas effectively. A good defensive team will alter its positions on the field to counter any offensive situation that might impair defensive efficiency.

There are times when the basic infield positions should be altered so that the infielders play closer or farther from home plate. These positions are called "back," "halfway," and "close in." The back position is taken when there is no one on base. The infield and outfield play back, or deep because the play probably will be to first base. This position enables the fielders to cover more territory. If the batter is left-handed, the infield and outfield shift about five steps toward the right-field line from their normal playing positions. The infielders play several steps behind the base paths.

The *halfway* or *pulled-in position* is assumed when there is a runner on first or second base with less than two outs. This position is also used when a bunt is expected or when the batter is a very fast runner. The halfway position allows for short, quick throws to prevent runners from advancing and also increases the possibility of a double play. In the halfway position, the outfielders move in a few steps, and the first and third basemen move several steps in front of the base path. The second baseman and the shortstop move in a step or two from regular position.

The *close position* is recommended when there is a runner on third base with less than two outs. This position enables the infield to field the ball rapidly so that they can hold runners on their bases or throw to home plate for an out. In the close position the outfielders move in a few steps, the first and third basemen move approximately one-third the distance from the base path toward home plate, and the shortstop and second baseman move to the base path. If the runner on third is the winning run, the outfielders move closer to the infield. If the fielding team is several runs ahead, however, some teams prefer to play back and attempt to make the surest out even though a run may score.

Defensive players not only must protect their areas but also must help the fielders nearest them whenever possible. If a base is not protected because the usual covering infielder is fielding the ball, the nearest available defensive player will "cover" the base. When a ball is being caught, the nearest available fielder moves to a position several feet behind the fielder making the play to be in position to stop the ball if it is missed. This is called *backing up the play*.

When a bunt is laid down, the pitcher, catcher, and first and third basemen come in to field it. The second baseman covers first base, the shortstop covers second base, and the third baseman returns to third immediately after the bunt is fielded. The right fielder backs up the first baseman, the center fielder backs up the second base, and the left fielder either backs up the third baseman or on occasion, in women's play, will cover third base. There are a variety of situations that require "covering and backing" by the defensive team. When there is a runner on first base with less than two outs and if the ball is

When should the fielding team assume the back position, the half-way position, and the close position shown in figure 7.1?

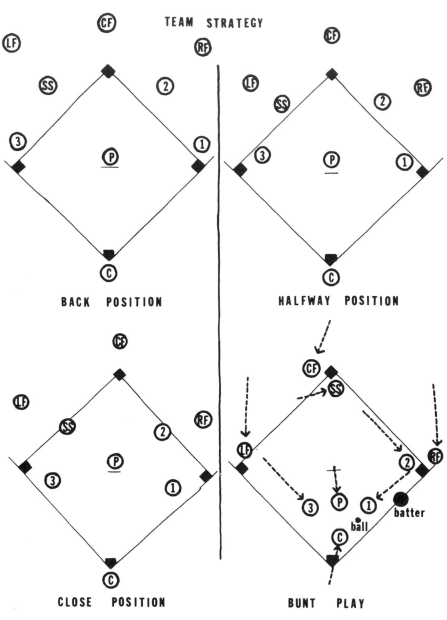

Figure 7.1   Defensive Positions

hit on the fly to left field, the center fielder backs up the left fielder, the right fielder backs up the second baseman and the pitcher backs up the first baseman. In the meantime, the first baseman covers first base and the second baseman covers second base. The shortstop moves toward the left fielder for a possible relay throw. The third baseman protects third, and the catcher covers home plate.

Pattern Errors and Corrections

Most pattern errors are the result of mental mistakes. The only possible correction is constant practice and extreme concentration by players. It is imperative that the team coach or manager constantly remind players, both on offense and defense, of possible actions that could and should occur. Teammates should shout directions and reminders to each other.

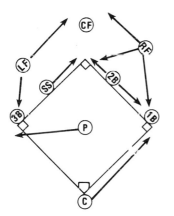

Figure 7.2   Covering and Backing

Play to first base; no runner on base. The catcher backs up the first baseman.

The second baseman covers first base when the first baseman must field the bunt.

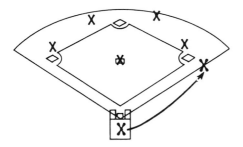

Figure 7.3   Catcher Backing Up a Play

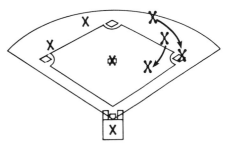

Figure 7.4   Covering First Base

When the second baseman must cover first base, the shortstop covers second base.

The pitcher covers home plate when the catcher is drawn away.

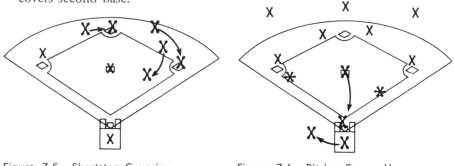

Figure 7.5   Shortstop Covering

Figure 7.6   Pitcher Covers Home

Shortstop backs up the second baseman when he covers the base, and the second baseman backs up the shortstop when he covers second base.

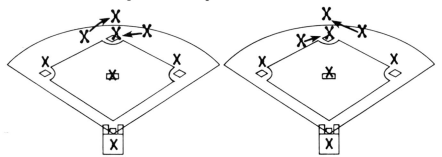

Figure 7.7   Action at Second Base

The pitcher covers first base when the first baseman must move to the right to field the ball.

The pitcher backs up the third baseman on plays to third base and backs up the catcher on throws to home plate.

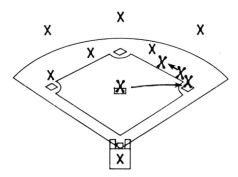

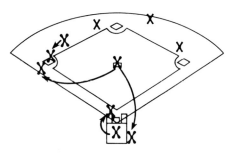

Figure 7.8   Pitcher Covering First Base

Figure 7.9   Pitcher Backing Up a Play

The right fielder backs up the first baseman, second baseman, and the center fielder.

The center fielder backs up the right fielder, left fielder, second baseman, and shortstop if necessary.

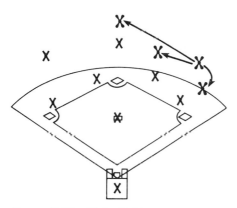

Figure 7.10   Right Fielder Backing Up a Play

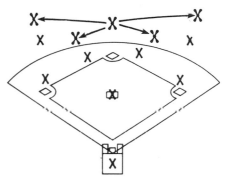

Figure 7.11   Center Fielder Backing Up a Play

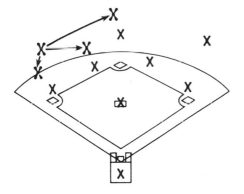

Figure 7.12   Right Fielder Backing Up a Play

The left fielder backs up the center fielder, third baseman, and shortstop if necessary.

Can you recall two restrictions placed on the slow pitch batter that do not apply to the fast pitch batter?

PRACTICE

Individual
Mental Practice   List possible playing situations and attempt to "think through" the play action that you should take from your playing position.

Group

Skill Sessions   The coach or team leader should list various playing situations, both offensive and defensive, and request that the team indicate what action they would take. Plays may be diagramed and given to players to study.

Mock Setups   Place the team on the field. The coach, manager, or team leader calls out or sets up various offensive situations for the defensive team to react to.

REFERENCES

DIAZ, LIVIA. "Hints on Backing Up." *1974-76 DGWS Softball Guide.* Washington, D.C.: American Association for Health, Physical Education and Recreation.

DOBIE, PAT. "Run Your Way to Victory." *1972-74 DGWS Softball Guide.* Washington, D.C.: American Association for Health, Physical Education and Recreation.

DOBSON, MARGARET, and SISLEY, BECKY. *Softball for Girls.* New York: Ronald Press, 1971. Chapters 10, 11, and 14.

HARRISON, PAT. "Thinking and Playing the Outfield." *1974-76 DGWS Softball Guide.* Washington, D.C.: American Association for Health, Physical Education and Recreation.

MOORE, JOHNNA. "Strategy of Baserunning." *1969 DGWS Selected Softball Articles.* Washington, D.C.: American Association for Health, Physical Education and Recreation.

WILSON, JANICE. "Tips on Infielding." *1972-74 DGWS Softball Guide.* Washington, D.C.: American Association for Health, Physical Education and Recreation.

Women's Softball. Mary Littlewood, consultant. Chicago: Athletic Institute. 1971.

ZWINGRAF, BETTY. "Defensive Plays." *1979-81 NAGWS Softball Guide.* Washington, D.C., National Association for Girls' and Women's Sports, American Alliance for Health, Physical Education and Recreation.

teaching, coaching, and managing
8

Your progress may be speeded up or helped if you are given expert assistance from a coach or manager, or you may speed up the progress of young players by utilizing effective instructional and management procedures.

Instructional Objectives

The learner will be able to—

1. plan and provide meaningful learning experiences,
2. improve the individual and team play of performers,
3. organize and conduct team play to maximize opportunities to win.

Respect for and acceptance of the coach are essential and are fostered through demonstrated knowledge of the game and firm but fair treatment of the players. A successful coach accurately diagnoses the needs of the player and prescribes meaningful learning experiences. In addition, good judgment, a sense of humor, and a positive self-concept are important personal traits that can inspire the desire to learn and the will to succeed.

PLANNING

Instructional plans are usually based upon the age, ability, and interest of the learner. Listed below is a suggested progression of skills for various age groups.

Ages 6 to 11	Ages 12–15	Ages 16 to Adult
Throwing	Batting: grips, bunting	Batting: hit-and-run, fake
Catching	Baserunning: leadoff,	bunting, drag bunting,
Fielding	stealing bases	place-hitting
Running	Throwing: overhand,	Baserunning: rounding, sliding
Batting	sidearm, underhand	Throwing: sidearm, cutoff

Ages 6–11	Ages 12–15	Ages 16 to Adult
Basic rules	Fielding: grounders, fly	Fielding: charging, reading
Leadup Games	balls, backing, use of	conditions
	mitt and glove, tagging	Strategy
	Position play: covering	Patterns of play
	area, duties	Official rules: advanced rules
	Official rules	Umpiring
	Slow-pitch game	
	Soft-softball fast-pitch	
	game	

TEAM SELECTION

You should select team members on the following basis: (1) apparent natural ability as demonstrated by ease and correctness when throwing, fielding, and hitting, (2) speed and hitting, (3) strong and accurate throwing, (4) dependability and dedication and (5) team needs. Although all of the above criteria are important, dependability and dedication can transform a below average player to acceptable abilities and vice versa.

COACHING AND MANAGING TECHNIQUES

As a coach or manager, you must have not only a thorough knowledge of your team but also of the opposition. This knowledge will assist you in deciding lineups, pitching changes, pinch hitters, runners, and fielding maneuvers. Decisions need to be made and communicated to the team concerning (1) their defensive positions, (2) where a play is to be made, (3) the likelihood of a bunt or steal, (4) plans to steal, and so forth. These decisions will be based upon a careful analysis of the following points:

Pitcher: control, style, "stuff," and fielding ability
Catcher: throwing ability, agility, alertness, and backing of first base
Infielders: position, throwing ability, covering, and backing excellence
Outfielders: field condition, speed, and throwing ability.

Promote improved play by reviewing the game with the team immediately after completion. Compliment good play but avoid placing blame and criticizing mistakes. Explain proper actions and prescribe special help and practice for consistent performance failures.

Use of Coaches

The rules permit one member of the offensive team to stand at the sidelines by first base and another by third base. These coaches may be players, coaches, managers, or other personnel connected with the team. They must not interfere with play, but they may direct the batting and running activities of the team.

The coaches shout words of encouragement to the batter and give the batter directions by the use of certain words or signs. Coaches assist the base runner in the proper running of the bases by shouting directions to them. A good coach must be able to make quick decisions. He assumes a position in the coach's box that will permit him to see the runners and fielders easily.

Safety

The following basic rules will help to ensure the safety of everyone playing softball.

1. Do not allow jewelry to be worn during play or practice.
2. Plan adequate warm-up time.
3. Arrange practice drills so that batted or thrown balls will not hit performers.
4. Arrange that each team is seated at least twenty feet behind home plate and behind the foul line.

PRACTICE

Individual and group practice drills and tasks have been suggested in earlier chapters. Maximize practice as much as possible. You should work with the learner to identify specific goals to be achieved.

The ball is batted over the left fielder's head. What signal should the first base coach be giving to the batter—base runner? Why?

Figure 8.1   Using Coaches

Drill Organization   Listed below is a suggested forty-five minute practice session:

Conditioning exercises	5-10 minutes
Review and practice skills	5-10 minutes
Plan individual and group tasks with identified goals.	
Introduce new skills (bunting)	5 minutes
Demonstrate, explain, and/or have available other input sources.	
Practice bunting	5-10 minutes
Work in groups of three. Hit five and rotate.	
Game play	15-20 minutes
Play bunt game.	

Team Organization   Preseason practice should begin four to six weeks before the schedule begins. Early meetings should stress conditioning, light throwing, and running. A typical practice session may be as follows:

Warm-ups and conditioning	15 minutes
Batting practice	60 minutes
Pitchers rotate every 20 minutes.	
Fielders play position and make directed plays.	
Batters are directed to hit a certain number of hits.	
Specific skill practice is conducted.	
Infield and outfield practice	45 minutes

REFERENCES

ALEXANDER, BETTY. "Teaching Softball Fundamentals: A Progressive Unit." *1969 DGWS Selected Softball Articles.* Washington, D.C.: American Association for Health, Physical Education and Recreation.

BLACKINTON, MARION. "A Method of Infield Practice." *1966-68 DGWS Softball Guide.* Washington, D.C.: American Association for Health, Physical Education and Recreation.

DOBSON, MARGARET, and SISLEY, BECKY. *Softball for Girls.* New York: Ronald Press, 1971.

HOWES, MARJORIE. "Principles of Base Coaching." *1969 DGWS Selected Softball Articles.* Washington, D.C.: American Association for Health, Physical Education and Recreation.

WALSH, LOREN. *Coaching Winning Softball.* Chicago: Contemporary Press, 1979.

rules and unwritten laws of the game

9

Instructional Objectives

The learner will be able to —

1. play softball according to the official rules,
2. understand and follow unwritten softball rules.

RULES OF THE GAME

All official rules, both fast- and slow-pitch, are under the jurisdiction of the International Joint Rules Committee on Softball. This committee is composed of representatives from the National Recreation Association, the American Alliance for Health, Physical Education and Recreation, the National Industrial Association, and the Amateur Softball Association. If an organiaztion wishes to publish the official rules, royalties must be paid to the International Joint Rules Committee on Softball. A complete set of rules can be secured from local sporting goods dealers, bookstores, or from your local library.

The Playing Field

Softball should be played in a clear and unobstructed area within a radius of 225 feet (male and female fast-pitch), 250 feet (female slow-pitch), and 275 feet (male slow-pitch) from home plate between foul lines, with unobstructed space beyond the foul lines at least 25 feet wide. The official diamond shall have 60-foot baselines. The pitching plate must be 40 feet from home plate for women and 46 feet for men. A batter's box that is 3 feet wide and 7 feet long is marked off on either side of home plate. A catcher's box and coaches' box must be marked off also. When deviations from these dimensions must be made, special ground rules may be agreed upon.

Players and Substitutes

A team shall consist of nine (fast-pitch) or ten (slow-pitch) players whose positions shall be designated as follows: pitcher, catcher, first baseman, second baseman, third baseman, shortstop, left fielder, center fielder, and right fielder. If a designated hitter is used in the fast pitch games, he becomes the tenth player. In the slow-pitch game, the tenth player shall be designated as a short fielder. Each player traditionally covers a certain specified area but may be stationed anywhere on fair ground except for the pitcher, who must be in legal pitching position, and the catcher, who must be in his box.

Substitute players may be used, but once removed from the game a player may not return. Substitute players may be put in the game for a batter, fielder, runner, or pitcher. The position of a player may be altered at any time during a game, but a substitute player must assume the position in the batting order of the player he replaced. However, in fast pitch play only, any of the *starting* players except the pitcher and "DH" (designated hitter) may be withdrawn and re-enter once, provided such player occupies the same batting position when he is in the lineup.

The Game

The home team bats last in each inning; however, if neither team is designated as a "home" team, the choice is determined by the toss of a coin. A game is complete when seven innings have been played. If the home team is leading, however, the last half of the seventh inning is not played. If the game should be tied at the end of seven innings, play continues until one side has scored more runs than the other at the end of a complete inning.

Occasionally a game cannot be completed because of weather, darkness, or calamities. In such cases, the decision to terminate the game is made by the umpire. If five or more innings have been played, the game is considered a regulation, completed game. A game may be forfeited by the umpire in favor of the team not at fault for failure to appear to play, for delaying or unduly hastening the game, for willful violation of a rule after warning, or for fewer than nine (fast-pitch) or ten (slow-pitch) players on a team.

The winner of the game is the team that scores the most runs in a regulation game. One run is scored each time a base runner legally touches each base consecutively before the third out of the inning.

Pitching Regulations

The game starts when the umpire calls "Play!" The first batter steps into the batter's box, the catcher readies himself in the catcher's box, and the pitcher stands with both feet firmly on the ground in contact with the pitcher's plate. He holds the ball in front of his body for not less than one second or more than twenty seconds. The pitch begins as soon as one hand is taken off the ball. The ball is thrown underhand. The pitch is completed when one step is taken toward the batter simultaneously as the ball is released. The pitcher may use any windup, provided he does not make any motion to pitch without immediately delivering the ball to the batter, use a rocker action, make more than one revolution of the arm, make any motion that results in a reversal of the forward action or continue to wind up after taking the forward step. In the slow-pitch game, the ball must be delivered at a moderate speed with a perceptible arc (from the time it leaves the pitcher's hand) of at least three feet before the ball reaches home plate.

When the pitch is delivered, the batter must decide if he wishes to swing the bat at the ball in an attempt to hit it. If the pitch is not struck at, the umpire decides whether the pitch is a ball or a strike. If the batter incurs three strikes, he is called out; conversely, if he acquires four balls, he is entitled to first base and becomes a base runner. If the pitcher delivers the ball illegally by dropping, rolling, or bouncing the ball to prevent the batter from striking it, or if he should use tape or other substances on the ball, a ball is called on the batter.

In the fast-pitch game only, base runners are permitted to advance one base.

Batting Regulations

If the batter elects to swing at the pitch and misses it, a strike is called. A foul ball is declared if the ball is hit but lands outside the lines defining the playing field. When a foul ball is not caught on the fly, a strike is called unless the batter already has two strikes. In this case he may hit any number of foul balls without a strike being called. A foul tip is called if the ball is hit by the bat and goes directly back to the catcher's hands and is held by the catcher. A foul tip is a strike regardless of the number of strikes on the batter. When a fly ball is caught, whether it is in fair or foul territory, the batter is out. If the batter hits the ball on the ground into fair territory, he must reach first base before the ball can be held by the first baseman while touching the bag, or he is declared out. Each team is given three outs during its time at bat. The batter is out when any of the following situations occur: when three strikes are called and the ball is held by the catcher; when a foul ball is legally caught; immediately when he hits an infield fly with base runners on first and second or first, second, and third bases with less than two out; or when he bunts the ball in foul territory when he has two strikes (fast-pitch only). The batter is out in slow-pitch softball if he chops downward on the ball or attempts to bunt the pitch.

Baserunning Regulations

The batter becomes a base runner as soon as he hits a ball into fair territory, or when four balls have been called, or when the catcher interferes with or prevents the batter from striking a pitched ball. In addition, in fast-pitch the batter becomes a base runner when he is hit by a pitched ball or when the catcher drops the third strike when no one is on base or in any situation when there are two outs. Bases must be touched consecutively. Two base runners may not occupy the same base. The right to a base is given to the runner who first occupied it, and he is entitled to hold that base until he has legally touched the next base or until he is forced to vacate it for a succeeding runner.

Baserunners are entitled to advance with liability to be put out when the ball leaves the pitcher's hand on a pitch (fast-pitch only), when the ball is overthrown into fair or foul territory and is not blocked, when the ball is batted into fair territory and is not blocked, and when a legally caught fly ball is first touched. In the fast-pitch game, leading off is legal. However, the base runner must return to his base if he does not steal once the pitcher has the ball within the eight-foot radius of the pitcher's plate.

Base runners are entitled to advance to another base and may not be put out in the following situations: when forced to vacate a base because the batter was awarded a base on balls, when a field obstructs the base runner's path, when the catcher interferes with the batter, and when a pitcher or overthrown ball in foul territory is blocked or obstructed. In addition, base runners may advance without being put out if the batter is awarded a base because he was hit by a pitched ball, when a wild pitch or passed ball goes under, over, or through the backstop, and when the pitcher pitches illegally.

There are times when a base runner is restricted to a certain number of bases. For example, if the fence is less than the prescribed distance from home base, a ball falling beyond it will entitle the runner to only two bases. If the fence is regulation distance, but the ball rolls or bounds into a stand or over, under, or through a fence or other obstruction marking the boundaries, two bases are awarded. When the team at bat commits an illegal act, a base runner cannot advance on the play. Thus, if a ball is illegally batted or if the batter interferes with a play, no advance is permitted. In order to protect the defensive team, if the umpire is struck by a batted ball before it is touched by a fielder or if the plate umpire interferes with the catcher's attempt to throw, no advance is permitted.

A base runner is declared out if he is not standing on a base and is touched by a fielder who is holding the ball or if he is forced to advance and fails to reach that base before the ball is held on that base by a fielder. A base runner also will be called out if he runs the base in reverse order, fails to return to his base when play is resumed after a suspension of play, passes a preceding base runner, leaves his base before a fly ball has been caught, fails to touch a base, is struck by a batted ball, or interferes with the fielding of a batted ball.

Officiating

The rules of the game are enforced by one or more umpires. They have the power to order a player or coach to act in any manner that, in their judgment, is necessary to give force and effect to one or all of the rules. An umpire must not be connected in any way with either team. If there are two umpires each has the power to make decisions on violations committed anytime during time or during suspension of play. One umpire rules from behind the plate and the other from the bases. The plate umpire has full charge and is responsible for the conduct of the game. He makes decisions on the pitches and the action of the batter. The base umpire renders decisions at all bases except at home plate. In tournament play, originally an umpire is assigned to each base.

Both the ASA and the NAGWS sponsor programs to prepare, assist, and regulate umpiring in softball. Questions concerning rules should be sent to

Can you run from home to first base in 4.2 seconds? 4 seconds? Can you run from home to second base in 7.6 seconds? 7.3 seconds? 7 seconds? Can you circle the bases in 16 seconds? 15 seconds? 14 seconds?

the International Joint Rules Committee on Softball official rules interpretor—Thomas J. Mason, 1000 S. Gerald Drive, Newark, Delaware, 19711.

Scorekeeping

The rules specifically outline procedures and regulations for scorekeeping. The official scorer records and summarizes the game activities as they relate to final score, runs batted in, hits, extra base hits, stolen bases, sacrifice bunts and flies, double plays, triple plays, runners left on base, bases on balls, strikeouts, wild pitches, passed balls, name of the winning pitcher, name of losing pitcher, names of umpires, and length of the game.

Sample Game

White City is playing Greenville at Greenville. Since Greenville is playing in its hometown, it is considered the home team and will bat last in each inning. The umpires arrive thirty minutes before the game in order to become familiar with the playing field and the teams.

Just before play begins, the umpires meet with the managers and team captains to go over ground rules. At the time designated to begin the game, the home team assumes its playing field positions. The visiting team bats first and in the order listed on the official batting lineup. The first batter hits the ball on the ground to the third baseman. He throws the ball to the first baseman who, while holding the ball, touches the bag ahead of the batter-base runner. This of course is an out. The next batter hits the ball over the shortstop's head; the ball lands before the left fielder can catch it. The left fielder knows that he cannot get the ball to first base before the batter-base runner, so he throws the ball to the second baseman to prevent the runner from taking an additional base. The next batter receives four balls and is given first base. The runner on first is allowed to take second base. On the next pitch, the batter hits a fly ball which is caught by the second baseman. There are now two outs. After taking two strikes, the sixth batter hits a ball that the center fielder drops for an error. The base runner on second scores on the error, and the batter-base runner gets to second base while the runner on first base stops at third. The last batter hits a foul ball that is caught by the catcher. This completes the first half of the first inning. The game continues in this manner until completed.

UNWRITTEN LAWS

Many softball procedures are accepted by players and fans alike, even though they are not listed in the official rules. Protesting close decisions made by the umpire, shouting words of encouragement, and taunting the opposition are acceptable. Players often follow certain superstitions and employ procedures and tactics that might delay or speed up the game.

Conduct of the Game

Protesting decisions is usually considered poor sportsmanship in most athletic endeavors but in softball such protests are accepted as part of the color of the game in nonschool game situations. No one really expects that a protest will result in a changed decision. Complaints are actually expected by fans, players, and officials. In educational settings, coaches and teachers should discourage adherence to the above unwritten law. Protesting too vigorously or using physical violence will result, however, in the offender's being ejected from the game by th umpire. This behavior is not considered sportsmanlike.

Shouting words of encouragement by teammates to the pitcher or the batter is expected and desirable. Occasionally disparaging remarks are made about the opposing pitcher or batter. These are not considered proper.

Stopping play to discuss the course of action to be taken is legal and is expected in certain situations. The manager may stop play to discuss offensive strategy with his batter, or he may choose to stop play to discuss defensive strategy when his team is in the field. Opposing fans usually boo mildly at these delays but cheer such delays when they are employed by their coaches. The rules limit conferences with the manager or other representatives from the dugout to one per inning.

Conferences occasionally are designed merely to delay the game for a psychological effect. A meeting of the pitcher and catcher is often held to give the pitcher a chance to calm down and rest or to "cool off" the opposition if they have been hitting the pitcher too frequently. The batter tries to annoy the picher by meeting with his coach or by stepping out of the batting box frequently.

Many players follow certain superstitions that they are certain affect the outcome of the game. For example, some players when running out to their defensive positions feel that they will have bad luck if they don't step on a certain base or hitch their belts before every new batter comes to bat.

MISCELLANEOUS LAWS

Rubbing dirt on the bat is done to dry perspiration so that the bat will not slip from the hands. The pitcher often uses rosin on his hands for the same reason.

The next batter to bat is said to be "on deck." When he is "on deck," he kneels halfway from the bench and plate, warmed up and ready to take his turn.

If the pitcher gets on base, play usually is stopped to give the pitcher his jacket. This is done to keep his pitching arm warm so it will not tighten up.

Throwing a bat is dangerous. Players should drop the bat and run to first base when the ball is hit. The bat should not be thrown unnecessarily or in anger.

Most teams wear uniforms to identify themselves. Men wear traditional baseball uniforms or slacks. Girls and women usually wear shorts and blouses.

REFERENCES

JACOBS, J., and McCRORY, J. R. *Softball Rules in Pictures.* 2d ed. New York: Grossett & Dunlap, 1969.

National Association for Girls' and Women's Sports. *Softball Guide.* Washington, D.C.: American Alliance for Health, Physical Education and Recreation, (published biannually).

Softball Rules Guide. Oklahoma City, Okla.: Amateur Softball Association, (published yearly).

playing the game
10

Softball provides action and excitement that may lead to awards and national and international recognition. Competition is provided on a local, regional, state, national, and international basis.

Instructional Objectives

The learner will be able to—

1. get into condition and improve his/her game performance,
2. find opportunities to play softball,
3. secure information about current softball developments.

SELF-EVALUATION

If you wish to develop skill as a softball player, you should know what skill looks like. Try to watch experts play. Read books or articles written about the position you play as well as about the game in general. Set batting, baserunning, and fielding goals for yourself. Know your batting average. You can figure it by dividing the total number of hits you have made by the total number of times you have been at bat. A batting average of .300 or more is considered excellent. Fielding average is computed by dividing your total putouts and assists by your total putouts, assists, and errors. A fielding average of .970 or better is considered excellent. Clock your running time from home to first and from home to the other bases. Constantly strive to improve that time.

No matter how much you know about softball or how much you practice, your progress toward increased ability in performing softball skills depends on how much effort and time you are willing to give.

How rapidly you master the skills of softball depends on many factors. Needless to say, every athlete would like to find a shortcut to the acquisition of skill. Most, however, would agree that there is no quick, simple way to stardom, but there are some steps that can speed up progress. The first step is to be in top physical condition so that you have the agility, endurance, and strength necessary to perform softball techniques. Conditioning is the foundation for perfecting skills. The real work is practice. Individual and group practice, faithfully pursued, will increase skill. In addition, a softball player must study the game and study himself. Only by knowing all the finer points of the game and understanding your own strengths and weaknesses can you intelligently progress toward real skill in playing softball.

CONDITIONING

To be an expert softball player you must possess arm and shoulder strength for throwing and batting. Endurance and speed are important to fielding and base-running. Timing, agility, and accuracy are necessary for batting and throwing. Exercise and practice should be pursued beyond the initial point of fatigue if improvement is to be expected. Exercises used for most sports have application to conditioning for softball. As in any sport, however, the exercises should relate to the specific sport. To improve shoulder strength, arm circling exercises could be done. Work up to enough arm strength to do up to fifty push-ups; modified push-ups are recommended for girls and women. Throwing a heavier ball several times daily will increase your arm strength. A ball can be made heavier by soaking it in water or wrapping tape around it. Increase the distance from the target when speed and accuracy are attained from a particular distance.

Endurance, leg strength, and speed can be developed by running or jumping rope. A softball player should work toward running at least four times around the field each day or jumping rope for fifteen to twenty minutes. Base-running is excellent for conditioning the legs for softball play. Stretching and bending exercises will improve flexibility and agility. Hand strength can be improved by squeezing a small rubber ball. Develop your own series of conditioning exercises and do them daily. Do not be content with merely doing the same amount each day. Set goals for yourself to improve your strength, speed, and the distance and accuracy of your throws.

COMPETITIVE PLAY

Softball competition begins with the friendly game at the park and ends with the World Softball Tournaments for men and women. Recently, softball has become a part of the Pan-American games. Between these extremes are intramural softball, interscholastic softball, church leagues, park leagues, and industrial leagues. Many teams are commercially sponsored.

The ASA is the governing body for nonschool-related competition. School competition is regulated by local school districts and state high school activity associations and is guided by the standards of the National Association for

---

Can you catch seven out of ten pop-ups? Ten out of ten? Fifteen out of fifteen?

Girls and Women's Sports. The Association for Intercollegiate Athletics for Women sponsors state, regional, and national championships.

One set of rules governs softball play for fast- and slow-pitch play all over the world. However, certain geographic areas or leagues may adopt special rules which become official *only* for that area. One outstanding variation, for example, centers in Chicago, Illinois. The sixteen-inch slow-pitch game permits base runners to lead off base and pitchers to use two hesitations before delivering the ball to the batter. During these hesitations, the pitcher may attempt to pick off a runner as in baseball. In addition, the bases are fifty-five feet apart, and the pitching distance is only thirty-five feet from home plate. Gloves or mitts are not permitted.

Any organization may form a league and sponsor competition whether it be a school, church, park, or industry. The league does not have to affiliate with the Amateur Softball Association unless it wishes to compete in the Amateur Softball Association tournaments. A group that wishes to compete with other highly skilled players should affiliate with the Amateur Softball Association and play on a statewide or nationwide level.

Membership in the Amateur Softball Association will provide a listing of affiliated teams and their locations, opportunity to participate in clinics, and assstance in local league organization and operation. A copy of the monthly newspaper, *Balls and Strikes*, is sent to members. The newspaper covers local, national, and world softball news. The ASA also publishes the official rules in a guide that contains playing rules, articles of general interest, photos, and statistics of world tournaments. This guide is also sent to members by the ASA.

All participants from the lowly sandlots to the championship playing field agree that softball brings enduring friendships, provides exercise, emphasizes good sportsmanship, and is good fun.

REFERENCES

Amateur Softball Association, Box 11437, Oklahoma City, Okla. 73125.
International Softball Federation. W. W. Kethan, Box 872, Pasadena, Tex. 77501.
National Association for Girls and Women's Sports. 1201 Sixteenth Street, N.W., Washington, D.C. 20000.

umpiring and scorekeeping
11

Quality softball play requires quality umpiring and scorekeeping. After learning about softball, you may wish to become an umpire or scorekeeper.

Instructional Objectives

The learner will be able to:

1. umpire softball games
2. keep score for softball games

UMPIRING

Umpiring is a difficult task but it can be enjoyable and rewarding. A thorough understanding of the rules governing play and umpiring, ability to maintain alertness and to exercise patience to enable consistent and accurate judgments are essential. Sponsoring agencies such as leagues, associations or tournaments usually set the minimum standards to govern the quality of umpiring for play. Obviously less rigor is demanded in "sandlot" play or in physical education classes than in inter-school, league, or tournament competition. Umpires are assigned to a particular game by the organizations they represent.

Number and Position of Umpires

The major function of umpiring of course is to enforce the rules as they related to batting, pitching, fielding and base running. The number of umpires used in a game depends upon the quality of play. Most games use two umpires. However, three umpires are recommended in tournament play.

Major duties are to judge the pitches, hits and render base decisions. When more than one umpire is used; one is called the plate umpire and the other, the base umpire. They both are enpowered to order the commission and omission of any act which in their judgment is necessary to comply to the rules.

General Information

The rules clearly identify the duties and responsibilities of umpires. Umpires are expected to wear uniforms consisting of powder blue shirts and dark navy blue pants. The plate umpire must wear a mask and body protector in Fast Pitch softball and their use is recommended in Slow Pitch play. In addition, the plate umpire needs a ball and strike indicator, a whisk broom and a ball bag. Each umpire should have a copy of the official rules available.

Umpires should confer with each other, coaches, managers and scorekeepers before the game begins. The plate umpire collects the games balls and returns them to the owner, and often checks the scorebook with the scorekeeper. All questions should be answered politely during and after the game. The following suggestions will contribute to quality umpiring:

1. Display dignified manner
2. Call plays consistently, fairly, promptly and accurately
3. Try to anticipate play in order to be ready for action.
4. Correct errors promptly
5. Avoid arguments and the making of personal comments
6. Be aloof and apart from players, coaches, managers and spectators.
7. Use signals and call out decisions loudly

Each umpire has the power to make decisions on violations committed at any time until the game is over. Neither umpire can set aside or questions decisions made by the other within the limits of their respective duties. Umpires may consult each other, but the final decision rests with the umpire whose exclusive authority it was to make the decision. All umpires have equal authority to call a runner out for leaving a base too soon, call TIME, remove players, coaches or managers, and call illegal pitches.

Plate Umpire

The plate umpire is considered to be the umpire in chief. As such he is in full charge for the proper conduct of the game. He positions himself one or two feet behind the catcher in a crouched position which will not interfere with the catcher or his ability to view the plate, batter, pitcher, foul lines, bases and field. Duties of the plate umpire are as follows:

1. Call balls and strikes
2. Call hit balls, fair or foul
3. Call legal or illegal pitches and catches
4. Call base play if the base umpire leaves the infield
5. Judge whether a ball is bunted, chopped, touches the batter or clothing of the batter
6. Judge a fly ball as in the infield or outfield
7. Determine when a game is forfeited
8. Assume all duties when assigned as a single umpire
9. Rule on fitness of field for play in case of rain or other problems.

Figure 11.1   Plate Umpire Position

Position   The plate umpire moves into a slight crouch when the pitcher steps in the rubber and assumes a readiness to pitch position. Eyes should be fixed on the pitcher and the ball. The body should be aligned with the pitch. Crouch lower, straighter or higher to align the body with the pitch. On a batted ball, the plate umpire takes a position in foul territory, no more than five feet down the baseline, in the direction of the next possible play. Umpires may rotate as provided in the rules.

Controlling the Game   The following procedures will contribute to a smooth and safe conduct of the game:

1. Encourage players to hustle on and off the field
2. Discourage lengthy conferences between players and/or coaches
3. Limit warmup pitches to five
4. Brush the plate between innings and at any other time when needed
5. Keep the field clear of debris, bats, loose material, and spectators
6. Keep "on deck" batter ready in designated waiting area
7. Suspend or discontinue play when the field or weather conditions present a hazard.

Base Umpire

The base umpire renders all decisions at bases except those made by the plate umpire. In addition, he shall assist the plate to enforce the rules.

Position   Because of the differences in leadoff and base stealing rules between slow and fast pitch softball, the position of base umpires vary somewhat. Details of these differences can be found in official umpiring manuals. Proper position of the base umpire changes with varying playing situations. When no

Figure 11.2 Base Umpire Position

one is on base, the umpire should stand ten to fifteen feet beyond the first base with the right foot beside the foul line in foul territory. If the ball is hit to the left side of the infield, the base umpire moves to fair territory ten to fifteen feet from first base and slightly outside of the first to second basepath facing first base. If the batter-runner advances toward second base, the base umpire moves toward the inside of the infield and stays with the runner. Generally, if the ball goes outside the infield, the base umpire must go inside of the basepath, and if the ball stays inside of the infield, the umpire stays outside of the basepath. If the ball is hit to the outfield, the umpire moves to a spot about five to feet to the infield side of the baseline between first and second base.

With runners on first base, the umpire moves to a position between first and second base, outside of the base path. The base umpire needs to maintain a position to have a good perspective of both the pitcher and baserunners. It is imperative that the position assumed does not obstruct the vision of an outfielder or impede the movements of an infielder. On a tag play, the umpire should be within five feet of the play and focus attention on the baseman, not the base.

Practice

Most organizations who sponsor or control league or tournament play provide clinics and workshops designed to develop and improve umpiring. The Amateur Softball Association and the National Association for Girls and Women's Sports promote clinics provide detailed information about umpiring and offer programs for official ratings. Attending of these events and assisting in less competitive games are excellent ways to improve ability in umpiring.

Do you know where to stand to umpire bases when a runner is on first base? If a ground ball is hit to the left side of the infield? If the batter-runner advances toward second base?

SCOREKEEPING

The scorekeeper should have a thorough knowledge of the rules and techniques of the games, ability to make decisions, and to attend to details.

The duties of the scorekeeper are to keep all records of each game as outlined in the official rules. It is the scorers responsibility to officially determine playing errors, base hits, runs batted in, pitching credit for winning or losing, stolen bases, passed balls, wild pitches. The scorer shall not make decisions which conflict with official playing rules or with the umpires decisions.

Signals

Most single decisions are indicated with both a visual and verbal signal.

Umpire Signals

Situation	Verbal Signal	Visual Signal
Begin or Resume play	Play Ball	Motion to pitcher
Strike	Strike	Raise right hand upward
Ball	Ball	No arm signal
Give Count	Call balls first	None
Foul Balls	Foul Ball	Extend arm horizontally away from diamond.
Fair Ball	None	Extend arm in a pumping motion toward the diamond.
Out	None	Raise right arm and hand over right shoulder with fingers closed.
Safe	None	Extend both arms diagonally in front of body with palms facing the ground.
Suspension of Play	Time	Extend both arms above his head.
Delayed Dead Ball	None	Extend left arm horizontally
Trapped Ball	None	Same as safe.
Ground Rule Double	None	Extend right hand above head with two fingers extended.
Home Run	None	Extend right hand with closed fingers above head and circle arm in clockwise direction.

Figure 11.3   Scorekeeper

Scoresheet   The scoresheet must be completed so that it is possible to reconstruct the official action of the game from which a box score and summary of the game can be prepared. There are many ways to record official action in a game. Some scorekeepers construct their own systems. Any system may be used providing game action is accurately recorded and can be retrieved by other readers.

Box Score   The box score should include each player's name and position and posititon and in the order in which he batted. The following information shall be recorded to each play: batting and fielding records including times at bats, runs, base hits, putouts, assists, entry and errors.

Summary   The summary of the game shall list the following information:

1. The score by innings and the final score.
2. The runs-batted-in and by whom hit.
3. Two-base hits and by whom hit.
4. Three-base hits and by whom hit.
5. Home runs and by whom hit.
6. Sacrifice flies and by whom hit.
7. Double plays and players participating in them.
8. Triple plays and players participating in them.
9. Number of bases on balls given by each pitcher.
10. Number of batters struck out by each pitcher.
11. Number of hits and runs allowed by each pitcher.
12. The name of the winning pitcher.
13. The name of the losing pitcher.
14. The time of the game.
15. The names of the umpires and scorers.

16. (FP ONLY) Stolen bases and by whom.
17. (FP ONLY) Sacrifice bunts.
18. (FP ONLY) The names of batters hit by a pitched ball and the name of the pitcher who hit them.
19. (FP ONLY) The number of wild pitches made by each pitcher.
20. (FP ONLY) The number of passed balls made by each catcher.

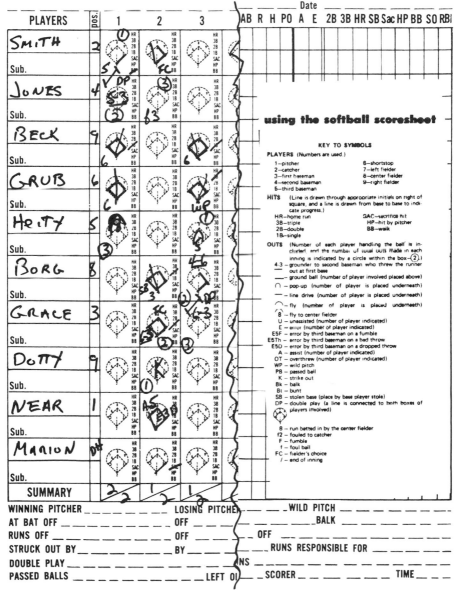

Figure 11.4   Scoresheet

EXPLANATION OF SAMPLE SCORESHEET

First Inning

Smith was walked (BB). Jones hit a grounder to the third baseman (5) who threw out Smith at second base on a double play (4) who tossed out Jones at first base (3). (Join Smith and Beck's boxes with a line ⊢———⊣) Smith ① and Jones ② were out. (outs are marked by number with a circle). Beck singled to right field (1B). Grub hit a home run (HR) over the center field fence (note line indicating area). Two runs were batted in by third baseman number 6 which is marked by (6) Heity hit a fly ball to center field ⑧ for the third out ③. 2 runs, 2 hits. 2/2.

Second Inning

Borg doubles (2B) to left field. Grace singles (1B) to right field, batting in Borg who had stolen third base (SB). Run batted in for Grace (3). Dotty struck out for the first out. (K) ①. Near was safe at first base on an error by the first baseman who dropped the throw from the third baseman (AF, E3D) Grace advanced to second base on a fielders choice (FC). Marion sacrificed Grace to third base (Sac). Smith grounded to the shortstop who threw Grace out at home plate ②. Smith was safe at first base on a (FC). Jones fouled out ③ to the first baseman (f3). One run, two hits. 1/2.

Third Inning

Beck singles to left field (1B). Grub tripled to right field (3B) scoring Beck. Run batted in for Grub (6). Grub scored on a wild pitch (WP). Heity popped out to the third baseman ⑤ for the first out ①. Borg was hit by a pitched ball (HP). Grace hit a grounder to the second baseman who throws out Borg at second base ②, 4-6, on a throw to the shortstop who throws out Borg at first base to complete a double play ③, 6-3. Two runs, two hits. 2/2.

Do you know how to keep score? What is meant by ⑤ ? ② ? 6-3?

REFERENCES

Amateur Softball Association, *Softball, A Game for Everyone*, Oklahoma City, Okla., 1977.

DOBSON, MARGARET, and SISLEY, BECKY. *Softball for Girls*. New York: Ronald Press, 1971.

National Association for Girls and Women Sport, *Softball Guide*, Washington, D.C., American Alliance for Health, Physical Education and Recreation. Published bi-annually.

Umpires Manual

questions and answers

1. Where is the best position for the second baseman to stand when no one is on the base?
   a. on second base
   b. between first and second bases, slightly closer to second base
   c. between first and second bases, slightly closer to first base
   d. between first and second bases, halfway between first and second base
   (p. 63)

2. Where should the first baseman stand when there are no base runners and the batter has two strikes?
   a. about six feet toward second base and about two to three steps behind first base
   b. with one foot touching first base
   c. with both feet straddling the base
   d. on the baseline, halfway between first and second base (p. 62)

3. When is a delayed steal most effective?
   a. with base runners on first and second base
   b. anytime
   c. with base runners on first and third base
   d. with bases full (p. 31)

4. Who is responsible for catching a fly ball falling between the infielders and outfielders?
   a. outfielders   c. whoever calls for it
   b. infielders   d. the fastest runners   (p. 68)

5. There are less than two outs with runners on first and second base. The batter hits a fly ball to the infield. What is the decision concerning the batter?
   a. becomes a base runner   c. automatically takes first base
   b. called out   d. continues to bat   (p. 87)

6. Where does the short fielder position himself in slow-pitch softball if the batter is a right-handed long ball hitter?
   a. in the infield near second base
   b. between the left and center fielder
   c. between the right and center fielder
   d. in the infield between the shortstop and second base
   e. between the infield and outfield and a bit to the left   (p. 69)

7. Who backs up the third baseman?
   a. left fielder   c. shortstop
   b. pitcher   d. catcher   (p. 78)

8. Who should back up the first baseman when a ground ball is hit to the third baseman with no base runners on base?
   a. pitcher   c. right fielder
   b. second baseman   d. catcher   (p. 77)

9. When playing fast-pitch softball, which procedure should be followed to pitch a curveball to the right?
   a. snap wrist to right   c. snap wrist down
   b. snap wrist to left   d. snap wrist upward   (p. 55)

10. What position should the infield be playing when there is a runner on third base with less than two outs?
    a. back position   c. close position
    b. halfway position   d. bunt position   (p. 76)

11. When may both fast- and slow-pitch baserunners advance to the next base but with liability to be put out?
    a. after a fly ball is caught   c. after ball leaves the pitcher's hand
    b. after a base on balls   d. anytime   (p. 88)

12. Which type of bat should be chosen for a tall, strong and well-coordinated batter?
    a. short and heavy   c. long and light
    b. short and light   d. long and heavy   (p. 16)

13. In fast-pitch play, where should the third baseman stand when a bunt is expected?
    a. behind base path   c. in front of base path
    b. on base path   d. halfway to home plate   (p. 75)

14. What regulations distinguish slow-pitch from fast-pitch pitching?
    a. moderate speed and at least a three-foot arch.
    b. no difference
    c. no deception
    d. only a three-foot arch   (p. 56)

15. What position should the infield be playing when there is a runner on first base and less than two outs?
    a. back position   c. close position
    b. halfway position   d. bunt position   (p. 75)

16. Where should a right-handed player attempt to contact the ball to place hit to right field?
    a. opposite the body   c. behind the body
    b. in front of the body   d. doesn't matter   (p. 19)

17. Which procedure should be followed to pitch a "drop" ball?
    a. snap wrist right   c. snap wrist down
    b. snap wrist left   d. snap wrist upward   (p. 55)

18. What name was given to softball when it was first developed?
    a. Kittenball   c. Rounders   e. Slow pitch
    b. One old cat   d. Bat ball   (p. 10)

19. Which athlete below is a member of the Softball Hall of Fame?
    a. Dizzy Dean   c. Jim Bunning   e. Lorene Ramsey
    b. Harold Gears   d. Helen Smith
                                                              (p. 12)

20. There are three balls and two strikes on the batter. The next pitch is bunted foul. What is the decision of the umpire?
    a. batter is out
    b. thecourt remains the name
    c. foul ball
    d. strike three   (p. 87)

21. The base runner leaves the base before the ball leaves the pitcher's hand. What is the umpire's decision?
    a. legal, base runner is safe
    b. illegal, base runner is out
    c. illegal, ball is called on the batter
    d. depends on what the batter does to the pitch   (p. 87)

22. A batted ball bounces in the infield and then rolls outside the baseline. What is the decision of the umpire?
    a. strike   b. out   c. fair ball   d. foul ball   (p. 87)

23. What is the minimum number of innings to be completed for an official game?
    a. seven
    b. six
    c. four
    d. five   (p. 86)

24. The batter has one strike and two balls when he tips the next pitch which is caught by the catcher. What is the decision of the umpire?
    a. strike   b. out   c. fair ball   d. foul ball   (p. 87)

25. The catcher drops the ball on the third strike. Bases are full and there is one out. What is the umpire's decision?
    a. strike   b. out   c. foul ball   d. ball   (p. 87)

26. Which player may not re-enter the game once in fast-pitch softball?
    a. pitcher
    b. catcher
    c. fielders
    d. no one   (p. 86)

27. What action should a right-handed batter take to "place hit' the ball to left field?
    a. contact ball opposite body and follow through naturally
    b. contact the ball a little past the center of body and follow through toward right field
    c. contact the ball anywhere over the plate and swing fast with a full follow-through
    d. contact the ball in front of the body, "break" wrists sharply to cause a forceful follow-through   (pp. 18-19)

28. Where is the strike zone?
    a. between the shoulders and ankles and over the plate
    b. no higher than the neck and no lower than the knees and over the plate
    c. between armpits and knees over the plate
    d. between armpits and the knees   (p. 2)

29. In fast-pitch softball, when may a base runner lead off base?
    a. as soon as the pitcher starts to throw the ball
    b. as soon as the catcher catches the ball
    c. as soon as the ball leaves the pitcher's hand
    d. as soon as the batter hits the ball   (p. 29)

30. How many bases may a base runner advance on an overthrow over the third baseman's head into fair territory?
    a. one   b. two   c. as many as possible   d. none of these   (p. 88)

31. What action should be taken to correct a tendency to strike out by missing the ball?
    a. shorten grip and watch the ball closely
    b. shorten grip and adjust stride
    c. lengthen grip and swing faster
    d. lengthen grip and adjust stride   (p. 24)

32. Which fast-pitch delivery makes a complete circle for the windup?
    a. straight pitch   b. slingshot   c. windmill   d. rocker   (pp. 32-33)

33. Where should the "on deck" player be located?
    a. on the bench
    b. halfway between outfield and first and third base
    c. halfway between bench and the plate
    d. doesn't matter   (p. 90)

34. What is the correct movement for a right-handed person in executing an overhand throw?
    a. stand with left shoulder toward person to whom the ball is going and step ahead on the left foot
    b. stand with the left shoulder toward the person to whom the ball is to be thrown and step ahead on the right foot
    c. stand facing the person to whom the ball is to be thrown and step ahead on the left foot
    d. stand any way that is comfortable and step ahead on either foot   (p. 44)

35. Where should the hands usually be placed on the bat?
    a. both hands close together at the end of the bat
    b. hands separated about two inches apart, but near the end of the bat
    c. hands separated, about three inches from end of the bat
    d. hands close together about two or three inches from the end of the bat
                                                                           (p. 17)

36. Which is the correct method to use in fielding ground balls?
    a. wait for the ball to roll to you
    b. run forward to meet the ball and try to field it on the first bounce
    c. run forward to meet the ball, but wait until the ball has slowed down to assist in stopping it
    d. creep up on the ball slowly.   (p. 37)

37. How should a fielder catch a fly ball that is going over his head?
    a. run backwards and keep eye on the ball
    b. wait until the ball has landed and then run to pick it up
    c. let the player behind you catch it
    d. turn around and run toward the direction the ball is headed, keep eye on the ball   (pp. 35-36)

38. How should the batting order be selected?
    a. let the team decide
    b. according to the positions played on the team
    c. according to the batting skill of the batters
    d. pitcher, catcher, then the weakest hitters next   (p. 74)

39. What is the term used for a batted ball that goes directly back toward the catcher and is caught?
    a. foul ball   b. foul fly   c. pop-up   d. foul tip   (p. 13)

40. Which grip on the bat is best to use in fast-pitch softball against a fast pitch?
    a. long   b. medium   c. choke   d. depends on the batter   (p. 17)

41. Which grip is used for power?
    a. long   b. medium   c. choke   d. depends on the batter   (p. 17)

42. How should the batter adjust his/her position when the ball leaves the pitcher's hand?
    a. relax   c. shift weight to rear foot
    b. hold position   d. shift weight to forward foot   (p. 18)

43. When playing fast-pitch softball, which type of pitch is easiest to bunt? (Right-handed batter)
    a. high outside   c. in the middle   e. high inside
    b. low outside   d. low inside   (p. 23)

44. What is the correct method to round a base?
    a. swing wide before reaching the base and touch any part of the bag
    b. run straight to the base, touch the inside corner and pivot body around
    c. curve out a bit several feet from the base and touch the inside corner
    d. get there any way possible   (p. 26)

45. Which slide is best to use to stop your speed, yet be able to recover fast enough to run again if it is possible?
    a. straight-in   b. bent-leg   c. hook   d. any of the above (pp. 27-28)

46. Which slide is best to avoid being tagged?
    a. straight-in   b. bent-leg   c. hook   d. any of the above   (6ᴢ ᵖ)

47. What position should your hands be in to field or catch a ball below your waist?
    a. thumbs together   c. left hand only, palm up
    b. little fingers together   d. hand with glove on it, facing upward
    (p. 39)

48. What is the correct position for fielding a ground ball? (Right-handed player)
    a. brace feet apart with left foot ahead, bend knees and hips
    b. bend only from the waist
    c. brace feet apart with right foot ahead, bend knees and hips
    d. bend from knees and hips only   (p. 37)

49. What is the best body position for a tag play?
    a. straddle the bag, place gloved hand in front of base
    b. stay to one side of base and tag runner
    c. brace feet apart behind the base and reach for the runner
    d. block the base with the left foot and tag the runner   (p. 39)

50. What is the advantage of an overhand throw?
    a. the throw can be done faster
    b. more accurate for a short distance
    c. speed and power are best
    d. throw can be delivered sooner   (p. 44)

TRUE OR FALSE

51. Softball has a greater appeal for general participation than baseball because the ball is soft.   (p. 3)

52. Aluminum bats are legal to use.   (pp. 5-6)

53. The pitcher should cover home plate and first base when the players usually protecting those positions are not there.   (p. 78)

54. The shortstop should cover third base when the third baseman is not there.   (p. 65)

55. To change "pace" is to vary the speed of the pitch.   (p. 13)

56. Groove is to throw the ball in a straight line.   (p. 14)

57. Coaches direct the batting and baserunning activities of the team at bat.   (p. 82)

58. A foul ball and a foul tip are the same thing. (p. 13)
59. It is legal for the pitcher to start to pitch and then stop. (p. 12)
60. The playing field for fast- and slow-pitch play is the same size. (p. 85)
61. If the pitcher hits the batter with a pitched ball, the batter is allowed to go to first base. (p. 87)
62. The only time a base runner must be tagged out is when he is forced to run. (pp. 87-88)
63. If a base runner is hit with a batted ball, he is out immediately. (p. 88)
64. If a base runner is hit with a thrown ball, he is out immediately. (p. 88)
65. The shortfielder in slow-pitch play may play either in the infield or the outfield. (p. 69)
66. The infield fly rule does not apply if the ball is dropped. (p. 87)
67. The catcher should wear a face mask at all times when catching the pitch. (p. 6)
68. Batters may not wear batting helmets in either slow or fast pitch softball. (p. 3)
69. One set of rules govern softball play for fast- and slow-pitch play all over the world. (p. 94)
70. Short fly balls between the infield and outfield are usually the responsibility of the infielders. (p. 68)
71. Fast pitch softball permits a designated hitter. (pp. 74, 86)
72. Pitching dominates fast-pitch softball when it is played by highly skilled players. (p. 2)
73. Softball is played extensively on a purely recreational basis. (p. 1)
74. The best bat is one that feels heavy. (p. 5)
75. The batter-base runner should watch the batted ball while running to first base. (p. 26)
76. Bunting is legal in both fast and slow pitch softball. (pp. 26, 87)
77. "Giving" with the catch will prevent the ball from bouncing out of the glove and hands. (p. 39)
78. When catching a ball thrown to a base, catching position should be delayed to the last second. (p. 38)
79. Only the finger pads touch the ball in the correct grip for a throw. (pp. 44-45)
80. A longer throw can be achieved by holding on to the ball longer. (p. 46)

COMPLETION

81. What player is the defensive leader? (p. 47)
82. What is the term applied to hitting to a certain spot? (p. 18)
83. What is the most commonly played version of softball? (p. 10)
84. What is the offensive play called with the base runner tries to advance at the same time the batter tries to hit the ball? (p. 20)
85. What two types of bunts are executed to achieve a base hit? (p. 21)
86. What is the term applied to a play that is interrupted or intercepted enroute to the intended receiver? (p. 47)

87. What is the name of the organization that promotes softball in the United States?   (p. 8)

88. What player backs up home plate on outfield hits with runners on base?
                                                                    (p. 78)

89. What kind of a hit will a level swing produce?   (p. 14)

90. What action must be applied to the swing to deaden the ball for bunting?
                                                                    (p. 20)

91. List three factors that would determine whether you should steal a base while playing fast-pitch softball?   (p. 30)

92. List two factors that will aid the fielder to immediately judge a fly ball. (p. 36)

93. List three kinds of pitches.   (p. 55)

94. Where should the infielders play when the bases are full?   (p. 75)

95. Where should the infielders play when the bases are empty?   (p. 75)

96. What is the term applied to gaining two outs on one batted ball? (p. 13)

97. What is the major purpose of a slide?   (p. 27)

98. What umpire is designated as umpire-in-chief?   (p. 96)

99. What is the visual signal that an umpire gives to indicate a "ball"?   (p. 99)

100. What is the name of the tenth player in fast-pitch softball who does not play defensively?   (p. 2)

ANSWERS TO EVALUATION QUESTIONS

Page	Answer and Page Reference
4	There are 9 players in fast pitch softball and a tenth player, short fielder, in the slow pitch game. More action is provided in the slow pitch game in which the ball must be delivered to the batter at moderate speed and with an arch. Stealing bases and bunting are legal in fast pitch but illegal in slow pitch softball. (pp. 2-3)
6	Aluminum bats are more durable and more uniform than wood bats. Aluminum bats can be manufactured in light weights without sacrifice in the diameter. (p. 6)
15	See pages indicated for definitions. (pp. 13-14)
20	The majority of the hits go toward left field. Adjustment of the timing of the swing does not signal your intentions to the defense, but a change in stance is a give-away. (p. 19)
21	The choke grip results in a shorter than usual hit. (p. 20)
21	If the body weight is already over the forward foot at the time of the hit, the smooth progression of movement is disrupted and the power contributed by the body weight is lost. (p. 18)
23	Self testing question.
24	Self testing question.
25	Self testing question.
30	Self testing question. The hook slide is used to avoid a tag by the infielder; the bent-leg slide is used to stop your speed at a base and to regain your feet immediately; the head first slide is used when there is much danger of being tagged. (pp. 28-29)

35   Self testing question.

38   The fielder "loops" by running a few steps behind where the fly ball is to be received in order to be moving forward at the time of the catch toward the base to which the throw is to be made. The technique is tried when there is a base runner and time permits.   (p. 36)

43   Self testing question.

55   Self testing question.

61   Low because the batter is well back in the box. The pitched ball can pass through the strike zone and then drop too low to be hit easily.   (p. 60)

64   Self testing question.

67   Field only with the glove hand, warm up with easy throws, catchers keep the throwing hand clenched until the catch; call out "It's mine" when another fielder might go for the ball but your position is better.   (pp. 39, 66)

68   Self testing question.

74   Self testing question.

76   Assume "back" position with no base runners; "halfway" position when there are runners on first or second base with less than two outs, when a bunt is expected, or when the batter is a very fast runner; and "close" position with a runner on third and less than two outs.   (p. 75)

79   The slow-pitch batter may not chop downward on the ball or attempt to bunt it.   (pp. 3, 87)

83   The coach should signal the batter-runner to continue to the next base since the long hit should allow enough time to get there safely.   (p. 83)

89   Self testing question.

93   Self testing question.

98   With a runner on first, stand between first and second base, outside of base path. On a hit to left infield, move to fair territory, 10-15 feet from first base, outside of base path. If batter-runner advances toward second base, move toward inside of infield and stay with runner.   (pp. 97-98)

102   Player number 5 hit a pop-up. There are two outs. The shortstop threw to the first baseman.   (p. 101)

QUESTION ANSWER KEY

Multiple Choice

1. b	6. e	11. a	16. c
2. a	7. b	12. **d**	17. c
3. c	8. d	13. d	18. a
4. a	9. a	14. a	19. b
5. b	10. c	15. b	20. a
21. b	26. a	31. a	36. b
22. d	27. d	32. c	37. d
23. d	28. c	33. c	38. c
24. a	29. c	34. a	39. d
25. b	30. c	35. d	40. c
41. a	46. c		
42. c	47. b		
43. b	48. a		
44. c	49. a		
45. b	50. c		

True or False

51. T	57. T	63. T	69. T	75. F
52. T	58. F	64. F	70. F	76. F
53. T	59. F	65. T	71. T	77. T
54. T	60. F	66. F	72. T	78. T
55. T	61. T	67. T	73. T	79. T
56. F	62. F	68. F	74. F	80. F

Completion

81. catcher
82. place hit
83. slow-pitch
84. hit and run
85. drag and push
86. cutoff
87. Amateur Softball Association
88. pitcher
89. line drive
90. give
91. speed, no. of outs, kind of batter, ability of defense, score
92. wind, crack of bat, speed of ball
93. curve, drop, fast, rise, knuckleball
94. halfway
95. back

96. double play
97. avoid tag
98. plate
99. none
100. designated hitter

index

NOTES

NOTES

NOTES

NOTES

NOTES